THE
PRINCETON
REVIEW

McGraw-Hill Reading

STANFORD 9
PREPARATION
AND PRACTICE

Primary 3

McGraw-Hill
School Division

This booklet was written by The Princeton Review, the nation's leader in test preparation. The Princeton Review helps millions of students every year prepare for standardized assessments of all kinds. Through its association with McGraw-Hill, The Princeton Review offers the best way to help students excel on the SAT-9.

The Princeton Review is not affiliated with Princeton University or Educational Testing Service.

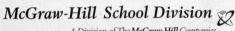

A Division of The McGraw-Hill Companies

McGraw-Hill School Division
Two Penn Plaza
New York, New York 10121

Printed in the United States of America

ISBN 0-02-185726-1

2 3 4 5 6 7 8 9 024 05 04 03 02 01 00 / 3

STANFORD 9
PREPARATION AND PRACTICE

Table of Contents

THE STANFORD 9

What is the Stanford 9?

The Stanford 9 (also called the SAT-9) is a multiple-choice test designed to find out what you have learned in school so far. Students from all over the country take the SAT-9.

Does the SAT-9 tell me how smart I am?

No, definitely not. The SAT-9 tests how well you can use the skills you've learned in class. As with anything else, the more you practice, the better you will perform.

Can I study for the SAT-9?

Studying for the SAT-9 will not help you get a higher score. However, you can go over the types of questions you will see on the test, and you can practice some simple test-taking techniques and tips for doing your best.

Why am I reading this book?

This book was made to prepare you for the SAT-9. It runs through each part of the test. It should be helpful for you.

What is in this book?

This book is a step-by-step tool made to prepare you for the SAT-9. It includes practice exercises to complete throughout the school year, a full-length Practice Test, and test-taking strategies for the SAT-9.

Will this book help me?

Yes, it will. This booklet will make you familiar with the types of question you'll see on the real SAT-9. By practicing with these types of questions, you'll know what to expect when you take the real test. And when you know what to expect, you are more confident and less likely to make mistakes.

Will this book help me get a better score?

By using this book, you certainly won't hurt your chances of getting a better score. To improve your score, however, you'll need to put some effort into the exercises. Pay close attention to the test-taking tips, and always ask your teacher when you don't understand something.

Preparing for the SAT-9

TIPS

✔ **Complete this book.** Complete the practice exercises throughout the year. Complete the Practice Test in class, just like you were taking the test for real. Learn the test-taking tips and techniques.

✔ **Practice the questions and sections that you think are the hardest.** Use test-taking techniques to answer these questions.

✔ **Practice doing some SAT-9 exercises while being timed.** The SAT-9 is a timed test. By doing this, you will practice in the same kind of conditions that you will have during the test.

✔ **Wear a watch to help you keep track of the pace of your work.**

✔ **Take the Practice Test seriously.** You'll be able to find out your strengths and weaknesses and change your habits before the day of the test.

✔ **Learn from your mistakes**. This book includes extra practice. Think about what is the hardest for you to do, and then give yourself extra study time for practicing these types of questions.

✔ **Don't be afraid to ask questions**. If you don't understand a question or an answer, ask your teacher.

✔ **Read books that challenge you.** Ask your teacher to help you pick a book that is at least one grade level ahead. When you come across a word that you don't understand, look it up in the dictionary.

✔ **Carry note cards with you**. Whenever you hear a word that is new to you, write it down and look it up later. This will help you build your vocabulary and reading comprehension skills.

✔ **Practice using word parts to figure out words.** You can often figure out the meaning of a word by concentrating on its root, prefix, or suffix.

✔ **Eliminate wrong answers.** If you don't know the answer to a question, eliminate as many answers as you can. Then guess! It's better to guess than to leave a question blank.

✔ **Practice good study habits.** Eat a good breakfast every morning. You can think better when you've eaten well. Also, take short breaks every now and then, to keep your mind refreshed.

✔ **Don't try to prepare for the whole test at once.** You will learn more if you only study one section of the test at a time. Focus on the parts of the test that cause you the most trouble.

Practice Exercises

Reading Vocabulary

DIRECTIONS

Look at the underlined word in each question. Then, choose the answer that is closest in meaning to the underlined word.

SAMPLE A

A A <u>rose</u> is a kind of—

Ⓐ office
Ⓑ flower
Ⓒ letter
Ⓓ snack

1 To <u>insist</u> is to—

Ⓐ plead
Ⓑ demand
Ⓒ borrow
Ⓓ guess

2 A <u>commotion</u> is a—

Ⓕ racket
Ⓖ train
Ⓗ highway
Ⓙ order

3 A <u>lecture</u> is a—

Ⓐ speech
Ⓑ letter
Ⓒ table
Ⓓ surprise

4 To <u>donate</u> is to—

Ⓕ change
Ⓖ break
Ⓗ give
Ⓙ steal

5 To <u>reject</u> is to—

Ⓐ play
Ⓑ ruin
Ⓒ share
Ⓓ refuse

6 <u>Gradually</u> means—

Ⓕ slowly
Ⓖ sweetly
Ⓗ timely
Ⓙ finally

7 Something that is <u>shriveled</u> is—

Ⓐ dried up
Ⓑ forgotten
Ⓒ broken
Ⓓ burnt out

8 To <u>prevent</u> is to

Ⓕ swell
Ⓖ miss
Ⓗ stop
Ⓙ loan

9 Something that is <u>bizarre</u> is—

Ⓐ hard
Ⓑ simple
Ⓒ messy
Ⓓ strange

DIRECTIONS

Use the words in the sentence to help you figure out the meaning of the underlined word. Then mark the space for your answer choice.

SAMPLE B

B Since this is a math test, I <u>advise</u> you to use a pencil. <u>Advise</u> means—

Ⓐ dislike
Ⓑ promise
Ⓒ recommend
Ⓓ argue

10 If you <u>observe</u> animals in the wild, you might notice that they act differently than they do in zoos. <u>Observe</u> means—

Ⓕ hear
Ⓖ smell
Ⓗ train
Ⓙ watch

11 Bill trained his <u>canine</u> to sit, to roll over, and to fetch a stick. A <u>canine</u> is a—

Ⓐ bird
Ⓑ mouse
Ⓒ friend
Ⓓ dog

12 Jon wanted to <u>ascend</u> the mountain so that hc could see the whole valley below. To <u>ascend</u> means—

Ⓕ climb up
Ⓖ scale down
Ⓗ read about
Ⓙ run around

13 We could not see the bottom of the river because the water was so <u>opaque</u>. <u>Opaque</u> means—

Ⓐ unclear
Ⓑ clean
Ⓒ fast
Ⓓ cold

14 After their big disagreement, Wanda and Maria <u>reconciled</u> and went back to being good friends. To <u>reconcile</u> means to—

Ⓕ meet with
Ⓖ play for
Ⓗ make up
Ⓙ yell at

15 My teacher's <u>recommendation</u> is that I study a little bit every day. A <u>recommendation</u> is—

Ⓐ an interest
Ⓑ a question
Ⓒ a suggestion
Ⓓ an idea

16 We cannot <u>preserve</u> your sick plant unless we water it and buy it more plant food. To <u>preserve</u> something means to—

Ⓕ lose it
Ⓖ see it
Ⓗ save it
Ⓙ love it

17 The <u>massive</u> statue reached so high into the sky that I could barely see the top. <u>Massive</u> means—

Ⓐ huge
Ⓑ quiet
Ⓒ old
Ⓓ beautiful

18 The hurricane looked so dangerous that everyone <u>evacuated</u> the town before it arrived. <u>Evacuated</u> means—

Ⓕ hid
Ⓖ prepared
Ⓗ left
Ⓗ returned

19 After the firemen <u>inspect</u> the area, they will find what started the fire. <u>Inspect</u> means to—

Ⓐ spray
Ⓑ examine
Ⓒ fill
Ⓓ drive

DIRECTIONS

Read the sample sentence inside the box. Then choose the answer that uses the underlined word in the same way as it is used in the example.

SAMPLE C

 Please <u>tape</u> the sides of the box so it does not open.

Which sentence uses the word <u>tape</u> in the same way as it is above?

Ⓐ I want to watch our <u>tape</u> of our summer vacation.
Ⓑ We need the electrical <u>tape</u> to fix this wire.
Ⓒ We need to <u>tape</u> up that rip in your costume.
Ⓓ Will you <u>tape</u> Channel 14 for me tonight?

 I like it when Dad decides to <u>drive</u> through the country.

Which sentence uses the word <u>drive</u> in the same way as it is above?

Ⓕ While playing golf the other day, Sally hit an incredible <u>drive</u>.
Ⓖ I really admire the <u>drive</u> with which you go after your goals.
Ⓗ Can you please <u>drive</u> Nancy to the park?
Ⓙ Every summer, Herman's family took a <u>drive</u> to Florida

---

21 **Why does Shelly keep asking what <u>time</u> it is?**

Which sentence uses the word <u>time</u> in the same way as it is above?

Ⓐ I know a lot about the <u>time</u> when the dinosaurs ruled the earth.
Ⓑ The exact <u>time</u> right now is 1:35 P.M.
Ⓒ Can you <u>time</u> me while I run around the track?
Ⓓ Clara kept <u>time</u> with the song by clapping her hands to the beat.

---

22 **By taking good notes, I have a <u>record</u> of what goes on in class.**

Which sentence uses the word <u>record</u> in the same way as it is above?

Ⓕ We had fun listening to my dad's old <u>record</u> collection.
Ⓖ Juan finished the crossword puzzle in <u>record</u> time.
Ⓗ I try to keep a <u>record</u> of everyone who has borrowed something from me.
Ⓙ The runner just set a new world's <u>record</u> in the last race.

---

23 **You told me to come to your house, but I do not know the <u>address</u>.**

Which sentence uses the word <u>address</u> in the same way as it is above?

Ⓐ As class president, I promise to <u>address</u> any problem that you may have.
Ⓑ Send the package to this <u>address</u>.
Ⓒ I try to be respectful when I <u>address</u> my elders.
Ⓓ The teacher told the class that we needed to take notes during her <u>address</u>.

---

24 **Would you rather <u>play</u> checkers or hide-and-seek?**

Which sentence uses the word <u>play</u> in the same way as it is above?

Ⓐ Before dinner, I usually go <u>play</u> outside.
Ⓑ Stan and Rashid are rehearsing for the school <u>play</u>.
Ⓒ Can I <u>play</u> the part of the lion?
Ⓓ Mr. Ronald told me that I <u>play</u> around too much.

---

25 In health class, we learned the importance of clean <u>air</u>.

Which sentence uses the word <u>air</u> in the same way as it is above?

Ⓐ The newspaper is a great place to <u>air</u> your opinions.

Ⓑ The radio announcer was not prepared to go on the <u>air</u>.

Ⓒ Open the windows so we can <u>air</u> out the apartment.

Ⓓ A chill in the <u>air</u> made me shiver.

26 My favorite <u>character</u> in the story was Ponche.

Which sentence uses the word <u>character</u> in the same way as it is above?

Ⓕ The letter "C" is the third <u>character</u> in the alphabet.

Ⓖ Donating money to charity displays <u>character</u>.

Ⓗ I don't remember the name of the main <u>character</u>.

Ⓙ You really are quite a <u>character</u>.

27 Do you have <u>space </u>in your room for the dresser?

Which sentence uses the word <u>space</u> in the same way as it is above?

Ⓐ The United States was the second country to launch a man into outer <u>space</u>.

Ⓑ In case you want to stay over tonight, we have plenty of <u>space</u>.

Ⓒ When people are angry, you should give them some <u>space</u>.

Ⓓ Let's <u>space</u> the chair and the couch two feet apart.

28 <u>Look</u> at that beautiful painting over there.

Which sentence uses the word <u>look</u> in the same way as it is above?

Ⓕ I don't like it when you give me that <u>look</u>.

Ⓖ I'll have to <u>look</u> for the information in my textbook.

Ⓗ When I <u>look</u> at you, I am reminded of my brother.

Ⓙ You <u>look</u> very nice today.

29 My math teacher always asks me <u>hard</u> questions.

Which sentence uses the word <u>hard</u> in the same way as it is above?

Ⓐ The sky got really dark, and we knew a <u>hard</u> rain was going to fall.

Ⓑ Reshod found himself in a <u>hard</u> situation when he had to choose between desserts.

Ⓒ The diamond is an example of a very <u>hard</u> gem.

Ⓓ I think Randy's parents are too <u>hard</u> on her.

Reading Vocabulary

DIRECTIONS

Read the sample sentence inside the box. Then choose the answer that uses the underlined word in the same way as it is used in the example.

SAMPLE A

The <u>main</u> idea of the story is to take care of yourself.

Which answer uses the word <u>main</u> the same way as it is above?

Ⓐ Becoming a writer is my <u>main</u> focus.

Ⓑ The city had a water <u>main</u> break.

Ⓒ Take a left at <u>Main</u> Street.

Ⓓ Gary is my <u>main</u> man.

Being able to <u>charm</u> people is quite a skill.

Which sentence uses the word <u>charm</u> in the same way as it is above?

Ⓐ Frank believes that no one can resist his grace and <u>charm</u>.

Ⓑ We watched the old man <u>charm</u> a snake just by playing a flute.

Ⓒ In the play we saw, an evil witch placed a <u>charm</u> on the princess.

Ⓓ My rabbit's foot is my good luck <u>charm</u>.

My sister has a <u>box</u> full of toys.

Which sentence uses the word <u>box</u> the same way as it is above?

Ⓕ We were seated in the <u>box</u> behind the players.

Ⓖ Remember to <u>box</u> the books for shipping!

Ⓗ I like to <u>box</u> in the gym.

Ⓙ A <u>box</u> is used for storage.

Is that little boy <u>lost</u>?

Which sentence uses the word <u>lost</u> in the same way as it is above?

Ⓐ We <u>lost</u> the race.

Ⓑ The army <u>lost</u> the battle.

Ⓒ My bicycle is <u>lost</u>.

Ⓓ Our TV was <u>lost</u> when it fell and broke.

That house is <u>mine</u>.

Which sentence uses the word <u>mine</u> the same way as it is above?

Ⓕ The soldier stepped on a <u>mine</u>.

Ⓖ These cookies are <u>mine</u>.

Ⓗ They had to dig a deep <u>mine</u>.

Ⓙ They found gold in the <u>mine</u>.

The train <u>station</u> is downtown.

Which sentence uses the word <u>station</u> the same way as it is above?

Ⓐ Where is the bus <u>station</u>?

Ⓑ We had to <u>station</u> ourselves around the camp.

Ⓒ A good soldier is always at his <u>station</u>.

Ⓓ That is my favorite radio <u>station</u>.

DIRECTIONS

Use the words in the sentence to help you figure out the meaning of the underlined word. Then mark the space for your answer choice.

SAMPLE B

B A <u>rose</u> is a kind of—

Ⓐ office

Ⓑ flower

Ⓒ letter

Ⓓ building

6 To <u>volunteer</u> is to—

Ⓕ offer

Ⓖ work

Ⓗ spend

Ⓙ confuse

7 Someone who is <u>kind</u> is—

Ⓐ caring

Ⓑ fast

Ⓒ strong

Ⓓ eager

8 A <u>quarrel</u> is a kind of—

Ⓕ stone

Ⓖ hat

Ⓗ soldier

Ⓙ fight

9 <u>Decrease</u> means to—

Ⓐ lessen

Ⓑ pretend

Ⓒ bother

Ⓓ struggle

10 Something <u>recent</u> is—

Ⓕ mean

Ⓖ new

Ⓗ soft

Ⓙ rare

11 <u>Combine</u> means to—

Ⓐ switch

Ⓑ miss

Ⓒ blend

Ⓓ prevent

12 To <u>quake</u> is to—

Ⓕ battle

Ⓖ shake

Ⓗ mix

Ⓙ slip

13 <u>Average</u> means—

Ⓐ common

Ⓑ steady

Ⓒ solid

Ⓓ more

14 To <u>glimpse</u> is to—

Ⓕ speak loudly

Ⓖ grow fast

Ⓗ look quickly

Ⓙ walk slowly

DIRECTIONS

Use the words in the sentence to help you figure out the meaning of the underlined word. Then mark the space for your answer choice.

SAMPLE C

C Since this is a math test, I <u>advise</u> you to use a pencil. <u>Advise</u> means—

Ⓐ dislike
Ⓑ promise
Ⓒ recommend
Ⓓ argue

15 A library will <u>loan</u> a book to you. <u>Loan</u> means—

Ⓐ sell
Ⓑ lend
Ⓒ throw
Ⓓ cook

16 She wanted to pour another glass of water, but the <u>carafe</u> was empty. <u>Carafe</u> means—

Ⓕ sink
Ⓖ pan
Ⓗ package
Ⓙ bottle

17 The singer's voice was so <u>shrill</u> that the windows rattled. <u>Shrill</u> means—

Ⓐ high and loud
Ⓑ brilliant
Ⓒ soft and deep
Ⓓ dreary

18 Our cat will <u>quiver</u> when it goes outside on very cold days. <u>Quiver</u> means—

Ⓕ nibble
Ⓖ purr
Ⓗ shake
Ⓙ sleep

19 The farmer keeps his cows in a <u>stable</u>. A <u>stable</u> is a—

Ⓐ truck
Ⓑ room
Ⓒ boat
Ⓓ barn

20 After a short break, we will <u>proceed</u> with the lesson. <u>Proceed</u> means—

Ⓕ stop
Ⓖ continue
Ⓗ turn around
Ⓙ struggle

21 The teacher may not use the room because it is <u>reserved</u> for another class. <u>Reserved</u> means—

Ⓐ broken
Ⓑ too small
Ⓒ saved
Ⓓ dark

22 The glass will <u>shatter</u> if you drop it. <u>Shatter</u> means—

Ⓕ get cloudy
Ⓖ break
Ⓗ bounce
Ⓙ dry out

23 The time on my watch doesn't <u>jibe</u> with the time on yours. <u>Jibe</u> means—

Ⓐ tick
Ⓑ talk
Ⓒ set
Ⓓ agree

24 Her father was so <u>gleeful</u> that he laughed aloud at silly jokes. <u>Gleeful</u> means—

Ⓕ jolly
Ⓖ skinny
Ⓗ alert
Ⓙ thoughtful

25 Instead of working alone, the students will <u>collaborate</u> to finish their projects. <u>Collaborate</u> means—

Ⓐ talk and listen
Ⓑ shake hands
Ⓒ work together
Ⓓ try hard

26 When you <u>submerge</u> the toy boat in the bathtub, bubbles rise to the surface. <u>Submerge</u> means—

Ⓕ put under water
Ⓖ float
Ⓗ rotate in the air
Ⓙ scrape

27 The coach <u>presented</u> the trophy to the winning team. <u>Presented</u> means—

Ⓐ threw
Ⓑ spoke
Ⓒ lent
Ⓓ gave

28 Jeff had to <u>reach</u> as far as he could to touch the top of the shelf. <u>Reach</u> means—

Ⓕ drop
Ⓖ throw
Ⓗ stretch
Ⓙ yell

29 Ron <u>rescued</u> the mouse before the cat could catch it. <u>Rescued</u> means—

Ⓐ saved
Ⓑ colored
Ⓒ washed
Ⓓ dropped

30 Plants grow in <u>soil</u>. <u>Soil</u> means—

Ⓕ air
Ⓖ leaves
Ⓗ dirt
Ⓙ paper

31 The car's <u>engine</u> would not start. <u>Engine</u> means—

Ⓐ tire
Ⓑ motor
Ⓒ truck
Ⓓ seat

32 The <u>clever</u> mouse got away from the cat. <u>Clever</u> means—

Ⓕ smart
Ⓖ fat
Ⓗ old
Ⓙ loud

33 The bug was so <u>tiny</u> we could not see it. <u>Tiny</u> means—

Ⓐ small
Ⓑ fast
Ⓒ mad
Ⓓ dirty

34 Tammy drew a box around the <u>borders</u> of the picture. <u>Borders</u> means—

Ⓕ tops
Ⓖ windows
Ⓗ couches
Ⓙ edges

35 Jen was <u>elected</u> class president in the vote. <u>Elected</u> means—

Ⓐ answered
Ⓑ picked
Ⓒ bought
Ⓓ taught

36 The floor was hard, so they sat on <u>cushions</u>. <u>Cushions</u> means—

Ⓕ rugs
Ⓖ coats
Ⓗ pillows
Ⓙ rocks

37 The angry <u>scowl</u> on his face showed that he was displeased. <u>Scowl</u> means –

Ⓐ eyes
Ⓑ frown
Ⓒ mustache
Ⓓ glow

STOP

Directions

Read each passage and answer the questions that follow.

Apple Harvest Fun Day

How Many Apples?

How many apples do you think there are in the barrel? Make a guess! The person who guesses closest to the actual number of apples wins. The winner gets an apple pie!

You must make your guess by one o'clock. The winner will be announced at two o'clock.

Directions

1   Look at the barrel of apples on the platform.

2   Guess how many apples are inside the barrel. You may talk about your guess or keep it secret.

3   Take an index card from the stack on the table.

4   Take a crayon or pencil to write your name on the card. Then use numerals to write your guess about the number of apples below your name.

5   Put your completed card into the slit on the cardboard box. You may put in only one card.

1 If your guess is closest to the number of apples in the barrel, you—

Ⓐ score a point

Ⓑ get to guess again

Ⓒ win a barrel of apples

Ⓓ win an apple pie

2 You would probably see this activity—

Ⓕ inside a museum

Ⓖ at a fair

Ⓗ on the beach

Ⓙ in a doctor's office

3 You can make your guess until—

Ⓐ one o'clock

Ⓑ two o'clock

Ⓒ three o'clock

Ⓓ four o'clock

4 The contest would be unfair if—

Ⓕ everyone was allowed to make two guesses

Ⓖ the apples were too large to fit in the barrel

Ⓗ a few kids used pens to write their names

Ⓙ a few kids counted the apples as they were put in the barrel

5 You can tell that the box is—

Ⓐ colored green so that it is easy to see

Ⓑ shut tight except for a small opening

Ⓒ too small for all the index cards

Ⓓ bigger than the barrel of apples

6 To decide the winner, the judges will—

Ⓐ look at the completed index cards

Ⓑ count the blank index cards

Ⓒ ask each person how many apples are in the barrel

Ⓓ see which kids kept their guesses secret

An Extra Day

Do you find it strange that every four years February has an extra day? We need that extra day because the earth does not go around the sun in an exact number of days. So every four years, we have a February 29th. What if you were born on that day? You would have to wait four years until your next birthday!

If we didn't have a leap year, the days would not come out right. Every four years, we would fall one day behind. For a while, you would not notice. But after many years, that time would add up. Someday, we would end up having cold weather on the Fourth of July and warm weather during the December holidays.

If we add an extra day every four years, the year comes out almost even. That way, the seasons will happen at the same time every year. But even adding an extra day every four years does not fix the problem completely. After 2000, years that end in 00 will not have an extra day. By taking away those extra days, the calendar will be even more accurate. Does this sound confusing? Don't worry, every four years will have the extra day until the year 2100. That is a long time from now!

7 How often does February have an extra day?

Ⓐ every 29 years

Ⓑ every year that ends in 00

Ⓒ every four years

Ⓓ every year until 2100

8 Why will years that end in 00 not have an extra day in the future?

Ⓕ calendar makers don't like those years

Ⓖ to make the calendar more accurate

Ⓗ they are a long time from now

Ⓙ to keep the earth going around the sun

9 Where could you find more information about leap years?

Ⓐ in a book about the earth and the sun

Ⓑ in a store that sells watches

Ⓒ in a story about snowmen

Ⓓ in a book about math

10 Which year has an extra day?

Ⓕ 2000

Ⓖ 2100

Ⓗ 2200

Ⓙ 2300

11 The point of this story is—

Ⓐ to get you to worry about the year 2100

Ⓑ to talk about the seasons

Ⓒ to explain why we have leap years

Ⓓ to explain how the earth revolves around the sun

Directions

Read each passage and answer the questions that follow.

Clyde the Squirrel Visits the City

Clyde was a country squirrel. He lived in the woods. His home was inside a hollow tree trunk. Every day he gathered seeds, berries, nuts, and buds. These are the foods squirrels eat.

One spring day, Clyde went to visit his cousin, Sid. Sid was a city squirrel. He lived in a small park near the City Square.

"Hello, cousin Sid," Clyde said.

"Hello, cousin Clyde," answered Sid. "Do you want to play?"

Clyde wiggled his tail. "Yes I do," he said. The two squirrels played in the park. They chased each other over rocks, around trees, and under park benches. After a while, they stopped near some children sitting at a picnic table.

"I'm hungry," said Clyde.

"I'm hungry, too," said Sid. "Let's gather some seeds and berries."

Just then, one of the children tossed something toward them.

"What is this?" asked Clyde. He had never seen a bright orange cheese curl before.

"Oh, that is a strange food that humans eat," said Sid. "We are squirrels. We eat seeds, berries, nuts, and buds."

Clyde decided to taste it. "Wow, this strange orange food is delicious," he said.

"It tastes good," said Sid, "but it is not healthy for a squirrel."

Clyde ate the rest of the cheese curl while Sid gathered some acorns.

When Sid returned, Clyde said, "My tummy feels a little upset."

"That strange food is not good for squirrels," said Sid. "Here, try an acorn."

Clyde ate the acorn. He began to feel much better. "I like squirrel food," said Clyde.

Sid replied, "Me too, cousin."

1 What did one of the children toss toward Clyde and Sid?

Ⓐ a berry

Ⓑ some seeds

Ⓒ a cheese curl

Ⓓ an acorn

2 The writer tells this story to show—

Ⓕ why squirrels like the country

Ⓖ that cheese curls taste good

Ⓗ that squirrels should eat squirrel food

Ⓙ why squirrels shake their tails

3 After Clyde's tummy felt better, Sid was probably—

Ⓐ sleepy

Ⓑ happy

Ⓒ afraid

Ⓓ bored

4 You can tell that this story did not really happen because—

Ⓕ squirrels cannot talk

Ⓖ animals do not live in cities

Ⓗ squirrels do not eat acorns

Ⓙ children cannot sit at picnic tables

5 Why did Clyde decide to taste the cheese curl?

Ⓐ Cheese curls were his favorite food.

Ⓑ He had never tried one before.

Ⓒ Sid tricked him.

Ⓓ He wanted to feel better.

6 Things that Clyde did are shown inside the boxes.

He went to the city.		He stopped near a picnic table.

What goes in Box 2?

Ⓕ He ate a cheese curl.

Ⓖ He said hello to Sid.

Ⓗ He tossed an acorn.

Ⓙ He ate an acorn.

The Father's Day Chef

Sherry was not the best cook. She would often spill things. But she still liked to learn about cooking. Sherry's older cousin Dee was a great cook. Together, Sherry and Dee made a pancake breakfast for Sherry's dad on Father's Day each year. They had now done it for the past three years. It became a tradition. Dee did all the pouring and measuring. Sherry did all of the stirring. They took turns flipping the pancakes.

This year would be different, though. Dee had moved away and could not come to Sherry's on the weekends. Sherry missed Dee. She needed her, too. How would she ever make a Father's Day breakfast without Dee's help?

Before long, Father's Day came around. Sherry woke up early and soon began work in the kitchen. She got out the flour, eggs, milk, and oil. Her mom found the baking powder for her. Sherry managed to mix all the ingredients without too many spills. Her mom poured some batter into the frying pan, but it was too thick. The first pancake was a dud. Sherry added a little water to the batter. Then her mom poured some more of it into the pan. Perfect! After bubbles formed around the sides of the pancake, Sherry's mom turned it over. It was golden brown! The whole kitchen smelled deliciously of pancakes.

Sherry glowed as she served breakfast to her dad. He said they were the best pancakes he had ever tasted.

That night, Sherry called Dee on the phone and told her what had happened. Dee told Sherry that she had become a terrific cook. She called Sherry a Father's Day Chef.

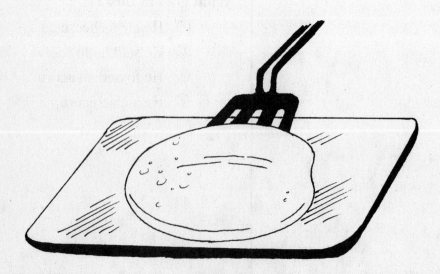

7 Which of these is another good title for the story?

Ⓐ "Sherry Makes a Special Breakfast"

Ⓑ "The Weekend Dee Came to Stay"

Ⓒ "How to Make Pancakes"

Ⓓ "The Pancake Twins"

8 What will most likely happen next?

Ⓓ Sherry will decide to stop cooking.

Ⓔ Sherry will thank Dee for calling her a chef.

Ⓙ Dee will become angry.

Ⓚ Dee's dad will ask for pancakes every morning.

9 Why did Sherry wonder if she could make the pancakes without Dee?

Ⓐ There was no one else who knew a good recipe.

Ⓑ Dee had the frying pan.

Ⓒ Sherry had never made pancakes without Dee.

Ⓓ Sherry didn't know how to flip a pancake.

10 Enough things happen in the story to show that Sherry was—

Ⓓ happy about the Father's Day breakfast she made

Ⓔ happy that Dee would not be spending weekends with her

Ⓙ sad because one pancake was not good

Ⓚ happy because the batter was thick

11 Why did Sherry add a little water to the batter?

Ⓐ The batter was too thin.

Ⓑ The batter was too thick.

Ⓒ There was not enough batter.

Ⓓ There was no milk.

12 Sherry's father thought that the pancakes were—

Ⓓ good, but salty

Ⓔ a little dry

Ⓙ not as good as Dee's pancakes

Ⓚ just right

Directions

Read each passage and answer the questions that follow.

Park Rangers

Who are the people that protect the parks? They are called park rangers.

They know a lot about nature and they have a big responsibility. They have to take care of plants, animals, and even people!

Park rangers get to spend most of the day outside. Park rangers are like the police of the park. Every day, they check the whole park to make sure everything is okay. What if a big tree falls down across a trail? Then they need to bring in a lumberjack to cut up the tree. What if someone is burning a campfire in an area where it is forbidden? The park rangers will have that person put out the fire!

Rangers also make sure that the animals are safe. Sometimes visitors try to feed the animals in the park. This isn't healthy for the animals. The ranger will ask the visitors to stop. Rangers make the parks safe for everyone and everything.

1 This was written to—

Ⓐ explain about a place

Ⓑ explain about a job

Ⓒ tell about the law

Ⓓ list some instructions

2 This story could also be called—

Ⓕ "Park Animals"

Ⓖ "The Lumberjack"

Ⓗ "Hiking in the Park"

Ⓙ "The Park Police"

3 Park rangers are—

Ⓐ busy

Ⓑ terrified

Ⓒ young

Ⓓ responsible

4 Why does the story tell about putting out the campfire?

Ⓕ to explain how it scares the animals

Ⓖ to tell how cold it is

Ⓗ to show how rangers protect the park

Ⓙ to show a park activity

5 Park rangers are usually—

Ⓐ inside

Ⓑ outside

Ⓒ in their car

Ⓓ by the campfire

6 A lumberjack is probably a—

Ⓕ tree cutter

Ⓖ park ranger

Ⓗ police officer

Ⓙ driver

7 To answer question number 6, you need to—

Ⓐ double-check the story's title

Ⓑ go back and read the first sentence in each paragraph

Ⓒ check the story for the word lumberjack

Ⓓ read the story's first paragraph

The Little Boat

Ana lived near the bay. All she had to do was to walk across the park to get to the water. She did this almost every day. Ana liked to watch the boats come and go. There were all kinds of boats! There were sailboats with big masts, which Ana usually saw on the weekends. There were big ships from faraway places. There was a ferry that traveled to the other side of the bay. If you wanted to go across the bay, you could ride the ferry. That was fun! The ferry had two decks. On the top deck, you could ride outside and watch the other boats go by.

Sometimes Ana saw a little boat. It was painted white, and it looked like it could fit only two people on it. Where did they go in such a little boat? One day Ana saw the little boat at a dock next to the park. A man and a woman sat in the boat. They were both wearing uniforms. "Why are you using that little boat? Why don't you use the ferry?" Ana asked.

"We are not out here for fun," the woman replied. "We are waiting for a ship to come in, so we can help it get to shore," the man said. "See? Here comes one now."

The little boat moved toward the big ship. It was huge! How could two people in a little boat help such a big ship? Ana stayed in the park and watched the big ship come close. The little boat moved to the side of the big boat and moved it closer to the pier. It really was helping the big boat! Ana saw the sign on the side of the little boat as it went by. It said "tugboat." Now Ana knew what it was doing on the water!

8 Ana did not know—

   Ⓕ who lived near the bay

   Ⓖ where the ferry went

   Ⓗ where the park was

   Ⓙ what the little boat was for

9 What does a tugboat do?

   Ⓐ watch for sailboats on the weekend

   Ⓑ helps big ships near the shore

   Ⓒ takes people across the bay

   Ⓓ travels to faraway places

10 Why did Ana go to the park?

   Ⓕ to watch the boats

   Ⓖ to help big ships

   Ⓗ to read signs

   Ⓙ to wear uniforms

11 When did Ana usually see sailboats?

   Ⓐ when the little boat was not around

   Ⓑ when she was on the ferry

   Ⓒ on the weekend

   Ⓓ when a big ship was in the bay

12 Why was this story written?

   Ⓕ to tell what the little boat was doing in the bay

   Ⓖ to describe who plays in the park

   Ⓗ to describe how many decks the ferry has

   Ⓙ to tell when sailboats are on the bay

STOP

Directions

Read each passage and answer the questions that follow.

Special Activities of the Month

Ms. Rey and Mr. Wilson's Art Class
Present

"Our Paintings"

A collection of ten paintings from each class

Main Lobby

Friday, October 29, 2:30 P.M.

Everyone is welcome.

Refreshments will be served.

Auditions

The dance and drama club is looking for actors and dancers for the Holiday performance of the Nutcracker. If you are interested, see Ms. Benjamin on Monday, October 18, or Tuesday October 19 at the Auditorium at 3:00 P.M.

Change of the Leaves Dance Party

School Gymnasium

Friday, October 15, 1999

5:30–8:00 P.M.

Students Free

Adults $2.00

Sponsored by the Music Club

and the Parents Association

Readings

Our English teacher, Ms. Steinberg,

will read her latest children's book,

Blue Bird

Wednesday and Thursday

October 20 and 21

at the Library

All Readings Held during

Lunch hours

1 Where will the party take place?

Ⓐ in the school library

Ⓑ in the school gymnasium

Ⓒ in the auditorium

Ⓓ the notice does not say.

2 Which day can a student go to the art exhibition?

Ⓕ Tuesday

Ⓖ Wednesday

Ⓗ Thursday

Ⓙ Friday

3 Who should the student see for acting tryouts?

Ⓐ Ms. Benjamin

Ⓑ Ms. Steinberg

Ⓒ Mr. Wilson

Ⓓ Ms. Rey

4 Which activity is not mentioned in the notices?

Ⓕ dance party

Ⓖ auditions

Ⓗ readings

Ⓙ Spelling Bee contest

5 Which event will happen last in the month?

Ⓐ the art exhibition

Ⓑ the acting and dance auditions

Ⓒ the dance party

Ⓓ the library readings

6 Where do you think these notices appeared?

Ⓕ in the *New York Times* newspaper

Ⓖ in an art magazine

Ⓗ on the school's bulletin board

Ⓙ on the supermarket's bulletin board

Growing Rice in Thailand

Thailand is a country in southeastern Asia. Many farmers in Thailand grow rice. Sometimes Thailand is called "Asia's rice bowl." It grows a large amount of rice and ships it to other Asian countries.

Most farmers in Thailand grow rice in fields called paddies. These flooded fields are a lot like shallow ponds. Tiny rice plants, called shoots, are stuck into the thick mud of the paddy by hand. The green rice shoots grow into tall stalks.

The rice stalks are ready to be gathered when they have a yellowish brown color. Farmers cut the stalks with sharp knives. Then they hang the stalks in the sun. After drying, the rough grains of rice are separated from the stalks. Some farmers use machines called threshers to make this job easier.

Next, farmers take the rough grain to rice mills. The outside cover on each grain of rice is then removed. The rice is polished and ready to be shipped all over Asia.

7 Farmers hang the stalks in the sun so that—

Ⓐ the stalks dry out

Ⓑ the stalks turn yellowish brown

Ⓒ the grains sprout

Ⓓ the rice can be planted

8 If you wanted to find out more about rice farming, you should—

Ⓕ read a cookbook

Ⓖ eat rice for dinner

Ⓗ visit a dairy farm

Ⓙ look in an encyclopedia

9 Farmers cut the stalks with—

Ⓐ threshers

Ⓑ rice shoots

Ⓒ sharp knives

Ⓓ short saws

10 Where are the covers of the rice grains removed?

Ⓕ in rice bowls

Ⓖ in paddy fields

Ⓗ in threshers

Ⓙ at rice mills

11 You would probably see this story in a book called—

Ⓐ *Cooking Rice*

Ⓑ *Farming in Asia*

Ⓒ *Pond Fishing*

Ⓓ *How to Build a Thresher*

12 After the rice is polished, it is—

Ⓕ shipped

Ⓖ threshed

Ⓗ cut

Ⓙ dried

STOP

Directions

Read each passage and answer the questions that follow.

If You See Reggie's Mother, Smile

Not long ago, Reggie moved to the city of Chicago with his mother and stepfather. Reggie's mother works as a dentist. Her dental office is on the ninth floor of a large medical building.

Reggie's mother likes being a dentist very much. She tells Reggie that the job takes a lot of work, but that it has many rewards. A dentist often works many hours in one day. A patient might have a bad toothache that needs to be treated right away. Patients trust that a dentist will give them the best care possible. A dentist makes sure that the mouth, teeth, and gums of each patient are healthy. When a patient has a problem, such as a cavity, a dentist fixes it.

Along with the dentist, other people work in a dentist's office. They all share the responsibility of giving patients the best care possible. Reggie's mother works in an office with three other people. The manager makes schedules and organizes all office activities. The dental assistant takes X-rays and keeps the dental equipment spotless. The hygienist cleans patients' teeth and shows people how to brush and floss.

Reggie's mother says that her favorite thing about being a dentist is working with children. She makes children comfortable by talking with them. Reggie's mother wants children to smile and to show their beautiful teeth.

1 Who takes X-rays and cleans dental equipment?

Ⓐ A manager

Ⓑ A dental assistant

Ⓒ A hygienist

Ⓓ A dentist

2 The story above was written to—

Ⓕ show you the size of buildings in Chicago

Ⓖ describe how a boy is treated by his mother

Ⓗ tell you about jobs in a dental office

Ⓙ show you how Reggie's mother makes kids laugh

3 To learn more about what a hygienist does, you should—

Ⓐ buy a toothbrush and some floss

Ⓑ read a book about the bones of the body

Ⓒ look for signs on a medical building

Ⓓ read a book about jobs in a dental office

4 The first paragraph answers which of these questions?

Ⓕ What does Reggie's mother like most about her job?

Ⓖ Where did Reggie move from?

Ⓗ Where does Reggie's mother work?

Ⓙ Where is the city of Chicago?

Figs for Sale

One day long ago, a man named Mr. Fox collected three figs. He tried to sell them near the town market.

Hours passed, but no one wanted to buy his figs. Mr. Fox was tired and sat down. Finally the good-hearted mayor of the town walked by and saw Mr. Fox.

The mayor stopped and removed his hat. "You look sad, Mr. Fox," he said.

Mr. Fox leapt to his feet. "I am selling sweet figs, sir. I have three tasty figs for sale."

"I would like to buy one fig," said the mayor. He pulled out a tiny white diamond from his pocket. "Will you accept this gem as payment?" he asked.

Mr. Fox's eyes widened. A diamond could buy a wagon full of figs inside the market. "Yes sir," said Mr. Fox.

Just after the mayor walked away, Mrs. Wise walked by.

"Mrs. Wise," said Mr. Fox excitedly, "do you know that the mayor is foolish? I am selling figs today. He paid me a diamond for a single fig."

"I like our good mayor," said Mrs. Wise.

Mr. Fox had an idea. "I will go inside the market and buy a wagon full of figs. Then I will sell each fig to the foolish mayor. He will pay me a diamond for each fig."

Mrs. Wise frowned. "I do not think that is a good idea."

"Why not?" said Mr. Fox.

"The good mayor is not foolish. He is kind. Do not become greedy, Mr. Fox. The mayor will not buy a wagon full of figs from you."

Mr. Fox looked at Mrs. Wise for a few moments. "You are right, Mrs. Wise. The good mayor is not foolish. He is kind. It was kind for the mayor to pay me a diamond for a single fig."

5 You can tell that the gem in the story was a—

Ⓐ fig

Ⓑ ruby

Ⓒ diamond

Ⓓ emerald

6 What will most likely happen next in the story?

Ⓕ Mr. Fox will go and thank the mayor.

Ⓖ Mrs. Wise will ask for the diamond.

Ⓗ The mayor will sell his fig.

Ⓙ Mr. Fox will buy a wagon full of figs.

7 Why did Mr. Fox say that the mayor was foolish?

Ⓐ The mayor wore a hat.

Ⓑ The mayor was good-hearted.

Ⓒ The mayor paid a diamond for a single fig.

Ⓓ Mrs. Wise liked the mayor.

8 Mrs. Wise knew that the mayor was—

Ⓕ foolish

Ⓖ hungry

Ⓗ tired

Ⓙ kind

9 When did Mrs. Wise walk by?

Ⓐ While Mr. Fox collected figs

Ⓑ Just after the mayor walked away

Ⓒ Before the mayor pulled a diamond from his pocket

Ⓓ After the town market closed

Directions

Read each passage and answer the questions that follow.

Ming's New Neighborhood

Ming stared out the window of his new bedroom. His family had just moved into a bigger house that was closer to town. Ming liked his new room. He was also glad that he didn't have to change schools. But Ming was afraid there wouldn't be anything fun to do in his new neighborhood.

Near his old house, there were wonderful places to play. A creek ran right through Ming's backyard. His old neighbors had horses that Ming helped to feed on weekends. His new neighborhood seemed to be filled with nothing but houses. Ming remembered a talk he'd had with his father. "There will be new places to play," his father had said. Now Ming wondered if his father was right.

The next morning was Saturday. Ming sat in the kitchen eating his second bowl of cereal. His father had woken up early to unpack some boxes.

"When you finish your breakfast, I'd like to show you something outside," his father said. Ming ate the rest of his cereal. Then he grabbed his jacket and followed his father out the front door.

"Where are we going?" said Ming.

"You'll see in about five minutes," his father replied, smiling.

They walked three blocks down the street. Suddenly, Ming saw a grassy field on the next block. Then he saw giant swings and all sorts of play equipment. There was even a baseball diamond, a water fountain, and a bike path. It was a huge, marvelous park.

"Wow, this is fantastic!" Ming said.

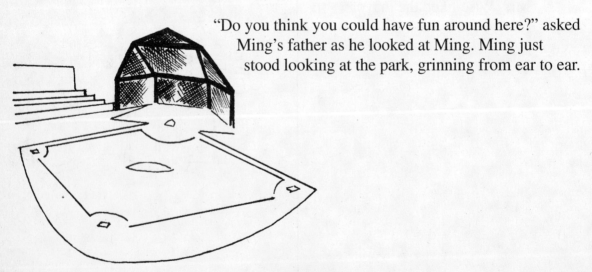

"Do you think you could have fun around here?" asked Ming's father as he looked at Ming. Ming just stood looking at the park, grinning from ear to ear.

1 Ming remembered something his father probably said—

   Ⓐ three or four years ago

   Ⓑ just before they moved

   Ⓒ while Ming was looking out the window

   Ⓓ while Ming was eating breakfast

2 Ming was afraid that—

   Ⓕ his new neighborhood would be boring

   Ⓖ he would have to change schools

   Ⓗ the new house would be too big

   Ⓙ his family would move again

3 What did Ming like about living in his old house?

   Ⓐ It was small.

   Ⓑ It was farther from town.

   Ⓒ There were good places to play nearby.

   Ⓓ His bedroom was better.

4 Why does the writer talk about the different things found in the park?

   Ⓕ to show that a good park must have fountains

   Ⓖ to tell why you can't see the park from Ming's house

   Ⓗ to show that a park is better than a creek

   Ⓙ to show why Ming thought the park was fantastic

Potato Ink Blocks

Here's a fun way to make ink blocks.

Gather these things:

Potatoes

A small knife

A cutting board

A marker

An inkpad

Some thick paper

A pen

Wash the potatoes. Have an adult cut them in half for you. Let the cut potatoes dry for about thirty minutes. As they dry, practice drawing designs on a piece of paper. If you want an ink blot with a name or word on it you will need to draw the letters backwards.

Draw one of your designs onto the flat side of a cut potato with a marker. Have an adult carve out the design for you with a knife. Repeat these steps for each potato. When you are finished, press the potato block onto an inkpad. Then stamp a piece of paper with the block. Let it dry for a few minutes. This is a great way to decorate a plain piece of paper.

5 An adult should help when you—

   Ⓐ want to draw the designs

   Ⓑ have to wash the potatoes

   Ⓒ need to cut the potatoes

   Ⓓ need to stamp the paper

6 How long do the potatoes take to dry?

   Ⓕ a few minutes

   Ⓖ they don't have to dry

   Ⓗ over night

   Ⓙ about thirty minutes

7 After gathering your materials, the first thing you do is—

   Ⓐ get a knife

   Ⓑ draw the designs

   Ⓒ bake the potatoes

   Ⓓ wash the potatoes

8 The inkpad is used for—

   Ⓕ putting ink on the cut potatoes

   Ⓖ drawing designs on the potatoes

   Ⓗ drying the potatoes

   Ⓙ holding the used ink blocks

9 You can find out how to do more activities like this—

   Ⓐ in a textbook

   Ⓑ in a crafts book

   Ⓒ in the kitchen

   Ⓓ at an art museum

STOP

Directions

Read each passage and answer the questions that follow.

Cricket Tunes

Chirp-chirp-chirp-chirp. Have you ever wondered about the sounds of the grasshopper's musical cousin? The cricket, a relative of the grasshopper, chirps beautiful songs.

The female cricket does not chirp. Only the male chirps. He makes a few different kinds of chirping songs by rubbing his front wings together. The "calling song" is the most common. He chirps to call any female crickets that can hear him. When a female cricket comes by, he chirps to her with a new song.

Both male and female crickets can hear the chirping songs. But the cricket does not have ears on its head. Instead, it hears through its front legs. Its legs work like the ears on your head. The cricket can hear very well.

1 **Where are the cricket's organs for hearing?**

Ⓐ on its head

Ⓑ under its front wings

Ⓒ on its front legs

Ⓓ under its ears

2 **The writer feels that chirping songs are—**

Ⓕ soft

Ⓖ silly

Ⓗ amusing

Ⓙ beautiful

3 **Why was this story written?**

Ⓐ to give instructions

Ⓑ to tell about an insect

Ⓒ to teach about the weather

Ⓓ to show a list of songs

4 **The "calling song" is used to—**

Ⓕ call female crickets

Ⓖ invite male crickets

Ⓗ say "hello" to grasshoppers

Ⓙ chirp when it is hot outside

5 **In order to find the answer to question 4, you should—**

Ⓐ look at the story title again

Ⓑ look for the words "calling song" in the story

Ⓒ read the first and last line of the story

Ⓓ read the last paragraph again

6 **Which title fits the story best?**

Ⓕ "Leaping Insects"

Ⓖ "The Grasshopper and the Cricket"

Ⓗ "Why Crickets Have No Ears"

Ⓙ "The Music of the Cricket"

A Hike to Buzzard's Peak

On Friday, May 3rd, Ms. Shen's class will go to Trader State Park. We will climb the park trail from the nature pavilion to Buzzard's Peak. Some of the trail is steep and narrow. Each child should wear sturdy, comfortable shoes or sneakers. Ms. Shen, Mr. Diaz, Ms. Richardson, and Principal Simon will supervise the trip. Parents/guardians must sign and return the permission slip below.

Schedule

10 A.M.–11 A.M.	Travel by bus from the school to the nature pavilion at Trader State Park
11 A.M.–12 noon	Hike two kilometers from the nature center up to Buzzard's Peak
12 noon–1 P.M.	Lunch at Buzzard's Peak
1 P.M.–2 P.M.	Hike two kilometers back down to the nature center
2 P.M.–3 P.M.	Tree identification at the nature center
3 P.M.–4 P.M.	Travel by bus from the nature center at Trader State Park to the school
4 P.M.	Parents must pick up their children at the school parking lot.

What to bring

1. A packed lunch

2. A liter of drinking water in a plastic water container

3. A sweater or jacket

4. A knapsack to put these into for the hike

(Cut along dotted line. Return the slip below to Mr. Diaz, the teacher's aide, by Tuesday, May 1st)

....

My child _____ has permission to go on the class trip. I will pick my child up at the school parking lot at 4 P.M.

_____

Parent/Guardian signs here

7 **Where will parents pick up their children?**

Ⓐ   At Buzzard's Peak

Ⓑ   At the school parking lot

Ⓒ   At Trader State Park

Ⓓ   The information sheet does not say.

8 **When will students begin to eat lunch?**

Ⓕ   11 A.M.

Ⓖ   12 noon

Ⓗ   1 P.M.

Ⓙ   2 P.M.

9 **The trail from the nature pavilion to Buzzard's Peak is—**

Ⓐ   uphill

Ⓑ   downhill

Ⓒ   level

Ⓓ   wide

10 **The permission slip should be returned to—**

Ⓕ   Ms. Shen

Ⓖ   Mr. Diaz

Ⓗ   Ms. Richardson

Ⓙ   Principal Simon

11 **If a student's parent wants to know more about the trip, the parent should—**

Ⓐ   walk to the nature pavilion

Ⓑ   ask a ranger at Trader State Park

Ⓒ   look in a history book

Ⓓ   call Ms. Shen

12 **Which item is not on the list of what to bring?**

Ⓕ   knapsack

Ⓖ   sweater

Ⓗ   blanket

Ⓙ   lunch

STOP

Directions

Read each passage and answer the questions that follow.

May's Flowers

Every spring, May's father planted a garden in the backyard. It was a beautiful garden and was full of delicious vegetables. This year he prepared more space than usual for the garden. May thought that he was going to plant something new this year.

May and her father went to buy the seeds together. She helped him pick out seeds for cucumbers, tomatoes, zucchini, carrots, corn, and May's favorite—snow peas. They bought these same seeds every year. May expected her father to buy some new seeds for the extra space he cleared. However, they did not buy anything unusual.

The next day, May and her father planted the seeds. They planted the corn near the fence. They planted the zucchini near the house. The carrots and tomatoes went in between. The snow peas went in the front. However, there was still a large, empty spot.

"Dad, are you going to plant anything in that spot?" May finally asked.

"Yes, but it's a surprise," he answered with a smile. "I think you will like what I plant there even more than you like snow peas!"

The next weekend, May and her father had fresh fruit and pancakes for breakfast. After they ate, May's father went down to the basement. He came back up with a small bag in his hand. He smiled at May, then went out to the garden. She followed him outside. She watched him plant the seeds one by one in a large circle. May was curious about the mystery seeds. When her father finally finished, he looked up at the blue sky. "Well, in a few weeks, you'll find out what your sunny surprise is."

They watered the garden every day. After a few weeks, everything began to sprout. May noticed that the ring of mystery seeds did not look like vegetables. They were fuzzy plants with skinny stems! They kept growing and growing. By the middle of the summer, they developed into sunflowers. Soon the sunflowers were even taller than May. When they were full-grown, she enjoyed standing in the middle of the patch and watching the wind sway the giant flowers around her.

1 **What was in the bag?**

Ⓐ sunflower seeds

Ⓑ cucumber seeds

Ⓒ trash

Ⓓ fresh fruit

2 **May thought it was strange that—**

Ⓕ her father planted a garden

Ⓖ she almost forgot snow peas

Ⓗ the garden was larger than usual

Ⓘ none of her friends had a garden

3 **Why did May follow her father outside?**

Ⓐ to avoid doing the dishes

Ⓑ to water the garden

Ⓒ to plant seed

Ⓓ to watch her father plant the mystery seeds

4 **They probably bought the seeds at a—**

Ⓕ restaurant

Ⓖ bookstore

Ⓗ grocery store

Ⓘ pharmacy

5 **What will May's father probably do next year?**

Ⓐ not plant a garden again

Ⓑ plant vegetables and sunflowers again

Ⓒ just plant sunflowers in his vegetable garden

Ⓓ just plant vegetables instead of sunflowers

You Can Make a Cloud!

What you will need

A large glass jar

A metal tray

A flashlight

A dozen ice cubes

Hot water

A dark room

What to do

Ask an adult to pour about an inch of hot water into a glass jar. Put the ice cubes on a metal tray. Set the tray on top of the jar. Turn out the lights or carefully take the jar into a dark room. Shine a flashlight toward the middle of the jar.

What happens

You will see a small cloud. You also see raindrops form on the bottom of the tray.

How it works

The hot water in the jar heats up the air in the jar. The warm air rises. The air contains invisible water vapor, or moisture. When the warm air hits the tray of ice cubes, the warm air quickly cools. This squeezes the moisture out of the air. The moisture turns into very small droplets of water. When enough droplets form, they become large enough to see. They form a cloud. When the drops become large and heavy, they fall as rain.

6 **Where do you put the ice cubes?**

Ⓐ in a glass jar

Ⓑ into hot water

Ⓒ on a metal tray

Ⓓ beside a flashlight

7 **What is the first thing to do?**

Ⓕ set the tray on top of the jar

Ⓖ get an adult to pour the hot water

Ⓗ turn out the lights

Ⓘ shine the flashlight into the jar

8 **You need the flashlight when you—**

Ⓐ look into the jar

Ⓑ find the ice cubes

Ⓒ put the ice cubes in the tray

Ⓓ pour the hot water

9 **What happens to the warm air when it reaches the tray of ice cubes?**

Ⓐ It heats up.

Ⓑ It cools quickly.

Ⓒ It expands.

Ⓓ It moves toward the flashlight.

10 **If you wanted to rename this activity, which title works best?**

Ⓕ "Clouds in the Sky!"

Ⓖ "Hot Water and Ice"

Ⓗ "Home-Made Cloud"

Ⓘ "Moisture Everywhere"

11 **If you wanted to do more projects like this one, you should—**

Ⓐ look in a science activities book

Ⓑ look in a children's cookbook

Ⓒ visit a park when it's raining

Ⓓ listen to a weather forecast

STOP

DIRECTIONS

Use the words in the sentence to help you figure out the meaning of the underlined word. Then mark the space for your answer choice.

SAMPLE A

A When Keisha got home from school, her mom greeted her with a warm <u>embrace</u>. An <u>embrace</u> is a—

Ⓐ breakfast
Ⓑ reply
Ⓒ hug
Ⓓ blanket

1 The electrician used a clip to <u>join</u> the two wires together. <u>Join</u> means —

Ⓐ connect
Ⓑ glue
Ⓒ point
Ⓓ paint

2 The cook used a big <u>ladle</u> to serve the soup. <u>Ladle</u> means —

Ⓕ plate
Ⓖ glass
Ⓗ spoon
Ⓘ fork

3 Ben had the good <u>notion</u> to see a movie last night. <u>Notion</u> means —

Ⓐ friend
Ⓑ idea
Ⓒ dream
Ⓓ feeling

4 Tina <u>plunged</u> perfectly into the pool from the high board. <u>Plunged</u> means —

Ⓕ tripped
Ⓖ bounced
Ⓗ danced
Ⓘ dived

5 We wanted to <u>select</u> a healthy puppy to be our new pet. <u>Select</u> means —

Ⓐ sell
Ⓑ choose
Ⓒ hide
Ⓓ rent

6 Mother used her best <u>urn</u> to serve the coffee whenever she had company. <u>Urn</u> means —

Ⓕ dish
Ⓖ cream
Ⓗ oven
Ⓘ pot

7 Once the police had them surrounded the bank robbers decided to <u>yield</u>. <u>Yield</u> means —

Ⓐ surrender
Ⓑ laugh
Ⓒ cry
Ⓓ travel

8 The parrot had to open its <u>bill</u> to speak or eat. <u>Bill</u> means —

Ⓕ cage
Ⓖ coat
Ⓗ beak
Ⓘ wings

9 The fox raises its family in a <u>den</u> that it digs in the ground. <u>Den</u> means —

Ⓐ stream
Ⓑ nest
Ⓒ forest
Ⓓ mountain

10 The teacher found the mistake on the test and <u>acknowledged</u> that the students were right. <u>Acknowledged</u> means—

Ⓕ settled
Ⓖ forwarded
Ⓗ pretended
Ⓘ admitted

DIRECTIONS

Look at the underlined word in each question. Then, choose the answer that is closest in meaning to the underlined word.

SAMPLE B

B To <u>repair</u> means to —

ⓐ do again

ⓑ notice

ⓒ destroy

ⓓ fix

11 To <u>flee</u> means to —

ⓐ escape

ⓑ aim

ⓒ throw

ⓓ lose

12 <u>Gentle</u> means —

ⓕ touch

ⓖ hard

ⓗ happy

ⓙ soft

13 To <u>compose</u> is to —

ⓐ write

ⓑ sing

ⓒ iron

ⓓ sit

14 Something that is <u>extra</u> is —

ⓕ alone

ⓖ a spare

ⓗ apart

ⓙ a tool

15 A <u>crate</u> is a —

ⓐ bag

ⓑ table

ⓒ couch

ⓓ box

16 A <u>label</u> is a —

ⓕ tag

ⓖ string

ⓗ price

ⓙ design

17 To <u>dodge</u> means to —

ⓐ run

ⓑ fight

ⓒ avoid

ⓓ think

18 Something that is <u>injured</u> is —

ⓕ asleep

ⓖ dead

ⓗ missing

ⓙ hurt

DIRECTIONS

Read the sample sentence inside the box. Then choose the answer that uses the underlined word in the same way as it is used in the example.

SAMPLE C

 The <u>main</u> idea of the story is that it is important to take care of oneself.

Which answer uses the word <u>main</u> in the same way as it is above?

Ⓐ Becoming a writer is my <u>main</u> focus.*

Ⓑ The city had a water <u>main</u> break.

Ⓒ Take a left at <u>Main</u> Street.

Ⓓ Gary is my <u>main</u> man.

 They used a <u>block</u> of wood to hold the tractor.

Which answer uses the word <u>block</u> in the same way as it is above?

Ⓐ Mary lives on our <u>block</u>.

Ⓑ Storms can <u>block</u> the television signal.

Ⓒ A cement <u>block</u> broke here.

Ⓓ The plumber needs to <u>block</u> the pipes.

 Father had to <u>light</u> a candle to see in the dark.

Which answer uses the word <u>light</u> in the same way as it is above?

Ⓕ Do you have enough <u>light</u>?

Ⓖ I can see better in this <u>light</u>.

Ⓗ We should <u>light</u> the fire.

Ⓙ These boxes are very <u>light</u>.

 We felt very <u>secure</u> after we bought a watchdog.

Which answer uses the word <u>secure</u> in the same way as it is above?

Ⓐ You must <u>secure</u> that rope tighter.

Ⓑ Dan used his credit card to <u>secure</u> a ticket.

Ⓒ Our money is very <u>secure</u> in the bank.

Ⓓ We can <u>secure</u> the door now.

 Because it was wrong the first time, he had to do it <u>over</u>.

Which answer uses the word <u>over</u> in the same way as it is above?

Ⓕ Please say the answer <u>over</u> again.

Ⓖ The trees towered <u>over</u> our heads.

Ⓗ My class is <u>over</u> for the day.

Ⓙ When will this movie be <u>over</u>?

 How did that old car <u>last</u> so long?

Which answer uses the word <u>last</u> in the same way as it is above?

Ⓐ Is this the <u>last</u> donut?

Ⓑ We can <u>last</u> until morning.

Ⓒ Where were you <u>last</u> night?

Ⓓ This is the <u>last</u> time I will tell you to stop.

24 The <u>bank</u> of the river was muddy.

Which answer uses the word <u>bank</u> in the same way as it is above?

Ⓕ You should put your money in a <u>bank</u>.

Ⓖ We tied our boat to a tree on the <u>bank</u>.

Ⓗ The <u>bank</u> of machines was as long as the building.

Ⓙ My little sister keeps her change in a piggy <u>bank</u>.

25 The <u>plot</u> of a story is the events which happen in it.

Which answer uses the word <u>plot</u> in the same way as it is above?

Ⓐ They have a small <u>plot</u> of land behind their house.

Ⓑ The bad men had a <u>plot</u> to rob the store.

Ⓒ This <u>plot</u> of forest belongs to my family.

Ⓓ The <u>plot</u> of that movie did not make sense.

26 The sound of voices surprised me and made me <u>spring</u> away from the door.

Which answer uses the word <u>spring</u> in the same way as it is above?

Ⓐ <u>Spring</u> arrives on March 20th this year.

Ⓑ The <u>spring</u> on the trap was tripped by the mouse.

Ⓒ That cat will <u>spring</u> into the air at the slightest noise.

Ⓓ The warm rain made it almost feel like <u>spring</u>.

27 The book was hard to read because the <u>print</u> was so small

Which answer uses the word print in the same way as it is above?

Ⓐ Will there be time to <u>print</u> another copy?

Ⓑ He wrote in <u>print</u> because that was easier to read.

Ⓒ The <u>print</u> on the paper smudged on my hands.

Ⓓ We need to get another <u>print</u> of the photo.

28 He tried to <u>block</u> the exit so that we could not leave.

Which answer uses the word <u>block</u> in the same way as it is above?

Ⓕ They planned to carve the <u>block</u> of marble into a statue.

Ⓖ I stepped onto the plastic <u>block</u> to reach the top shelf.

Ⓗ The simple wooden <u>block</u> was actually a table.

Ⓙ The flooded river is going to <u>block</u> our path.

Reading Vocabulary

DIRECTIONS

Use the words in the sentence to help you figure out the meaning of the underlined word. Then mark the space for your answer choice.

SAMPLE A

A Lisa forgot her umbrella and got <u>drenched</u> in the rain. <u>Drenched</u> means —

- Ⓐ dressed
- Ⓑ soaked
- Ⓒ lost
- Ⓓ sick

1 As the clouds clear, the sun will <u>emerge</u>. <u>Emerge</u> means —

- Ⓐ fade
- Ⓑ set
- Ⓒ appear
- Ⓓ retreat

2 Her eyelids <u>droop</u> when she gets sleepy. <u>Droop</u> means —

- Ⓕ hang down
- Ⓖ turn color
- Ⓗ keep secret
- Ⓙ object

3 We painted the outside walls and many of the <u>interior</u> walls. <u>Interior</u> means —

- Ⓐ large
- Ⓑ inside
- Ⓒ narrow
- Ⓓ crooked

4 The bear is <u>insulated</u> from the cold by thick fur. <u>Insulated</u> means —

- Ⓕ protected
- Ⓖ pushed
- Ⓗ drawn
- Ⓙ startled

5 The mechanic will <u>scrutinize</u> every part of the engine to see what is broken. <u>Scrutinize</u> means —

- Ⓐ turn on
- Ⓑ look at
- Ⓒ repair
- Ⓓ ignore

6 The <u>massive</u> rock covered the wide pathway, and we could not get by it. <u>Massive</u> means —

- Ⓕ bright
- Ⓖ bumpy
- Ⓗ huge
- Ⓙ round

7 After our neighbors moved, the house next door was <u>vacant</u>. <u>Vacant</u> means —

- Ⓐ bigger
- Ⓑ busy
- Ⓒ empty
- Ⓓ lucky

8 Little pieces of <u>tattered</u> flag still flew over the fort, even though the battle had been long and hard. <u>Tattered</u> means —

- Ⓕ ragged
- Ⓖ red
- Ⓗ fringed
- Ⓙ small

9 We tried to <u>persuade</u> him to stay by giving him a list of 10 Very Good Reasons. <u>Persuade</u> means—

- Ⓐ suspect
- Ⓑ flatter
- Ⓒ conceal
- Ⓓ convince

DIRECTIONS

Read the sample sentence inside the box. Then choose the answer that uses the underlined word in the same way as it is used in the example.

SAMPLE B

 I like to roll down the hill.

Which sentence uses the word roll in the same way as it is above?

Ⓐ I had a roll and butter for breakfast.

Ⓑ Roll up your sleeves before you wash the dishes.

Ⓒ I am on the honor roll at school.

Ⓓ We like to roll the ball back and forth.

 The coach told the team to keep practicing.

Which answer uses the word keep in the same way as it is above?

Ⓕ They had to keep swimming or they would drown.

Ⓖ May I keep this toy?

Ⓗ The cows slept in their keep.

Ⓙ You should always keep your money in a bank.

 Our forces will march into battle tomorrow.

Which answer uses the word forces in the same way as it is above?

Ⓐ The forces of nature can be dangerous.

Ⓑ The cowboy forces the cattle into the corral.

Ⓒ The enemy forces fought well.

Ⓓ No one forces Sheila to do anything.

 The kite lifted into the air, letting the colorful tail stream behind it.

Which answer uses the word stream in the same way as it is above?

Ⓕ The mighty river trickles down into a small stream by the time it reaches the highway.

Ⓖ As soon as the game was over, crowds of people began to stream out of the stadium.

Ⓗ The steady stream of voices soon turned into a flood of words.

Ⓙ There was a small stream of juice dripping from the half-frozen carton.

 I am tired, so I will take it easy.

Which sentence uses the word take in the same way as it is above?

Ⓐ There's no rush, so I will take my time.

Ⓑ Life is full of give and take.

Ⓒ How much money did he take you for?

Ⓓ Take a deep breath.

 I will fold laundry tonight.

Which sentence uses the word fold in the same way as it is above?

Ⓕ In some card games, you must either continue or fold.

Ⓖ These are the kind of chairs that can fold.

Ⓗ Mom, will you fold my pants before I put them away?

Ⓙ My dog's ears fold back.

DIRECTIONS

Look at the underlined word in each question. Then, choose the answer that is closest in meaning to the underlined word.

SAMPLE C

C To <u>repair</u> means to —

Ⓐ do again
Ⓑ read again
Ⓒ break up
Ⓓ fix up

15 Someone who is <u>bashful</u> is —

Ⓐ sweet
Ⓑ shy
Ⓒ cheerful
Ⓓ smart

16 <u>Tense</u> means —

Ⓕ tough
Ⓖ fair
Ⓗ weak
Ⓙ tight

17 A <u>limb</u> is a —

Ⓐ branch
Ⓑ flag
Ⓒ badge
Ⓓ poem

18 To <u>hesitate</u> is to —

Ⓕ give
Ⓖ wish
Ⓗ mark
Ⓙ pause

19 A <u>cluster</u> is a —

Ⓐ plate
Ⓑ flower
Ⓒ fish
Ⓓ group

20 <u>Uneasy</u> means —

Ⓕ difficult
Ⓖ lazy
Ⓗ nervous
Ⓙ slow

21 A <u>fable</u> is a kind of —

Ⓐ cloth
Ⓑ wish
Ⓒ story
Ⓓ song

22 To be <u>cautious</u> is to be —

Ⓕ careful
Ⓖ quiet
Ⓗ mean
Ⓙ hopeful

23 To <u>express</u> is to —

Ⓐ watch
Ⓑ join
Ⓒ show
Ⓓ erase

24 To <u>inquire</u> is to —

  Ⓕ beg

  Ⓖ ask

  Ⓗ borrow

  Ⓙ correct

25 If you are in <u>debt</u>, you —

  Ⓐ owe something

  Ⓑ need something

  Ⓒ feel tired

  Ⓓ feel sad

26 To <u>apologize</u> is to

  Ⓕ say you're sorry

  Ⓖ go home

  Ⓗ say thank you

  Ⓙ go quietly

27 If you are <u>cheerful</u>, you are —

  Ⓐ late

  Ⓑ last

  Ⓒ daring

  Ⓓ happy

28 <u>Unique</u> means —

  Ⓕ new

  Ⓖ fair

  Ⓗ large

  Ⓙ original

29 Something that is <u>murky</u> is —

  Ⓐ sweet

  Ⓑ smooth

  Ⓒ dark

  Ⓓ rare

30 To <u>consent</u> is to —

  Ⓕ agree

  Ⓖ seize

  Ⓗ spare

  Ⓙ mix

31 A <u>barrier</u> —

  Ⓐ confuses you

  Ⓑ stops you

  Ⓒ carries you

  Ⓓ keeps you warm

32 To <u>emerge</u> is to —

  Ⓕ leave

  Ⓖ come out

  Ⓗ grow

  Ⓙ switch

33 To <u>predict</u> is to —

  Ⓐ suspect

  Ⓑ foresee

  Ⓒ sigh

  Ⓓ fail

STOP

Directions

Read each passage and answer the questions that follow.

A Saturday Surprise

Hector lived in a big city. Mr. Kenny, a close family friend, lived across the hall in the same apartment building. Early one Saturday morning, Mr. Kenny came over. He was holding the handlebars of a green bicycle. He said that his son had outgrown the bike. He asked if Hector would like to have it.

"Gosh, yes," said Hector. "There's only one problem. I don't know how to ride it."

"How about learning right now," Mr. Kenny said. Hector's mother handed her son a brand new bike helmet. She already knew that Mr. Kenny was going to give Hector the bike!

Hector and Mr. Kenny walked to a playground nearby. Hector felt funny. He was excited, but he was also a little nervous. He got on the bike. The seat was at the perfect height for Hector. Mr. Kenny told him to pedal slowly. "Try to get your sense of balance," he said to Hector.

Hector pedaled around on the playground. Mr. Kenny ran alongside him, holding the back of the seat. When Hector got his balance, Mr. Kenny let go of the seat. Hector rode a little way and then put his foot down. Once Hector fell off the bike. "That didn't even hurt!" he shouted to Mr. Kenny.

They practiced for more than an hour. Hector started getting comfortable. He started going farther. Then, during one try, he just kept on pedaling. "You can feel it," he said. "You can feel it when you're balanced!" He rode across the playground and turned around in a circle. Mr. Kenny was smiling. Hector kept pedaling. "I'm doing it," he said. "I'm riding a bike."

1 You can tell that Hector's mother already knew about the bike because—

Ⓐ she let Hector go outside

Ⓑ she gave Hector a new helmet

Ⓒ she said it was green

Ⓓ she wanted Mr. Kenny to teach Hector

2 Why did Mr. Kenny hold the back of the bicycle seat?

Ⓕ He did not want Hector to move forward.

Ⓖ The seat was loose.

Ⓗ He was trying to lift the back wheel.

Ⓙ He did not want Hector to fall off the bike.

3 This story has enough information to show that—

Ⓐ Hector's mother made lunch for Mr. Kenny

Ⓑ Hector's mother trusted Mr. Kenny

Ⓒ Hector never fell off the bike again

Ⓓ Hector did not like Mr. Kenny

4 Which of these titles best fits the story?

Ⓕ "Hector Learns to Ride a Bike"

Ⓖ "Bicycles are for Bullies"

Ⓗ "Hector Meets Mr. Kenny"

Ⓙ "The Green Bicycle"

5 Hector felt funny because he never—

Ⓐ went to the playground before

Ⓑ spoke to Mr. Kenny before

Ⓒ saw the green bicycle before

Ⓓ rode a bicycle before

Hunting the Monster Flower

The largest flower in the world grows in the rainforests of a small part of Southeast Asia. The scientific name of this plant is *Rafflesia arnoldii*. It's also called the monster flower. That's a good nickname. The biggest monster flower ever measured was huge. It was ninety centimeters across and weighed eleven kilograms. That's over twenty-four pounds and three feet wide.

The monster flower grows on the ground of the forest. The center of the bloom is surrounded by five red petals. The flower looks pretty, but it smells awful. The bad smell attracts flies, which help the plant.

The monster flower is a strange plant. It has no stems, leaves, or roots. It is a parasite. It feeds on other plants. The monster flower has little threads that grow into the roots and stems of forest vines. This way it steals their food.

The monster flower is a rare plant. Finding the giant is not an easy task. The flower is the only part of the plant that you can see. It blooms for about a week only once or twice a year. To find the world's largest flower, you must look for it at just the right time.

6 Another good title for this story would be—

   Ⓕ "Flycatcher of the Forest"

   Ⓖ "Hunting and Fishing in Asia"

   Ⓗ "The World's Largest Flower"

   Ⓙ "The Most Beautiful Plant on Earth"

7 Why was this story written?

   Ⓐ to teach about a plant

   Ⓑ to show the way people used to live

   Ⓒ to tell you how to grow something

   Ⓓ to ask you for information

8 In this story, a <u>parasite</u> is a plant that—

   Ⓕ smells foul

   Ⓖ grows very large

   Ⓗ lives on vines

   Ⓙ feeds on other plants

9 To find the answer to question 9 what should the reader do?

   Ⓐ Read the last sentence of the story again.

   Ⓑ Find the word <u>parasite</u> in the story.

   Ⓒ Search for the scientific name of the plant.

   Ⓓ Look at the first paragraph of the story.

10 Why does the writer say how long the flower blooms for?

   Ⓕ To explain why it grows on the ground

   Ⓖ To show that it is huge

   Ⓗ To show that it is hard to find

   Ⓙ To show that it has no leaves

STOP

Directions

Read each passage and answer the questions that follow.

Mrs. Leary's Flower Vase

Before today, Mia never had a problem in Mrs. Leary's classroom. Some kids thought that Mrs. Leary was too strict. She did have a stern voice. She didn't seem to smile too often. Mia always thought that Mrs. Leary just didn't smile because of her crooked front teeth. But Mia couldn't say for sure that Mrs. Leary was nice.

Mia's daily job in Mrs. Leary's classroom was to empty the pencil sharpener. It was attached to the wall above a countertop, where Mrs. Leary kept her favorite flower vase. The short blue vase was a gift to Mrs. Leary from the teachers at her old school. When Mia removed the cover from the pencil sharpener, it slipped from her hand. The cover bounced high off the counter and hit the vase. It was chipped!

Just then, Mrs. Leary told everyone to sit down. Class was about to begin. Mia sat down and spent most of the lesson thinking about the vase. How would she tell Mrs. Leary? What would Mrs. Leary do?

When the math lesson ended, Mia's classmates went to lunch. Mia stayed behind. She took Mrs. Leary back to the pencil sharpener. She told her exactly what had happened. She said she was sorry for breaking the vase.

"I'm very proud of you for telling me," said Mrs. Leary. "Don't you worry about it another minute."

"Then I'm not in trouble?" asked Mia quietly.

Mrs. Leary asked Mia to sit down. She explained that Mia didn't break the vase on purpose. She wasn't being careless either. There was nothing to be in trouble for. It was just an accident. Mrs. Leary smiled at Mia with her crooked teeth. Mia smiled back. "Mrs. Leary *is* a nice teacher," she thought.

1 What class lesson took place after Mia broke the vase?

   Ⓐ Language Arts

   Ⓑ Science

   Ⓒ Math

   Ⓓ Lunch

2 Why did Mia stay behind when her classmates went to lunch?

   Ⓕ She wanted to ask about the lesson.

   Ⓖ Mrs. Leary asked her to stay after class.

   Ⓗ She was going to ask to go home early.

   Ⓙ She wanted to tell Mrs. Leary what happened.

3 Mia thought that Mrs. Leary didn't smile much because—

   Ⓐ she had crooked teeth

   Ⓑ she didn't like their class

   Ⓒ she was strict

   Ⓓ she missed her old school

4 If the story continued, what would Mrs. Leary probably do next?

   Ⓕ Ask Mia to pay for the vase

   Ⓖ Go over the math lesson again

   Ⓗ Tell Mia not to empty the pencil sharpener anymore

   Ⓙ Tell Mia to go enjoy her lunch

5 Why wasn't Mrs. Leary angry about the vase?

   Ⓐ She never really liked it.

   Ⓑ It was just an accident.

   Ⓒ Mia always did well in math.

   Ⓓ She could still use it.

Cartoonists

You have laughed at them in the newspaper. You have watched them on television. You have even played with them in video games. They are cartoons—funny drawings of people or animals. The artists who draw all these cartoons are called "cartoonists."

Since cartoons tell stories with pictures, a cartoonist must be both a good artist and a good storyteller. Cartoons are usually funny, but sometimes they are serious. Some cartoonists specialize in certain subjects, like action heroes or families. You do not have to have a formal education or training to become a cartoonist. However, only the most talented and dedicated people will become successful. Most cartoonists work in art studios. They can set their own work hours, but they usually have to meet difficult deadlines. That means that they have to finish a cartoon before a certain date.

A special kind of cartoonist is an <u>animator</u>. In the past, animators drew many individual pictures. Then they put the separate pictures together to make animated, or moving, cartoons. Now it is more common to use computers to do this. However, it still takes a lot of talent and skill to be an animator or cartoonist.

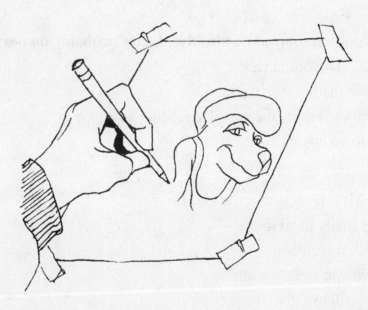

6 An <u>animator</u> is a special kind of—

   Ⓕ video game

   Ⓖ cartoonist

   Ⓗ scientist

   Ⓙ politician

7 The author believes that cartoonists are—

   Ⓐ funny

   Ⓑ serious

   Ⓒ strange

   Ⓓ talented

8 This story could also be called—

   Ⓕ "The History of Cartoons"

   Ⓖ "The Best Animated Movies"

   Ⓗ "Making a Movie"

   Ⓙ "A Special Kind of Artist"

9 The purpose of this story is to—

   Ⓐ talk about a job

   Ⓑ explain a hobby

   Ⓒ tell about different types of cartoons

   Ⓓ show how to play a game

10 Where do most cartoonists work?

   Ⓕ At a factory

   Ⓖ In an art studio

   Ⓗ At a computer company

   Ⓙ At a newspaper company

11 Why does the author mention action heroes and families?

   Ⓐ Because they are serious subjects

   Ⓑ Because all cartoonists like these subjects

   Ⓒ To show examples of subjects that cartoonists specialize in

   Ⓓ To compare them to cartoons

12 To see how the job of being an animator has changed, you should—

   Ⓕ read the last paragraph again

   Ⓖ read the first paragraph again

   Ⓗ check the title of the story

   Ⓙ look up the word <u>animator</u> in the dictionary

STOP

Directions

Read each passage and answer the questions that follow.

The Seventh Planet

The seventh planet from the sun has rings around it. Do you know its name? It is not Saturn. It is Uranus.

Unlike the rings of Saturn, the rings of Uranus are very hard to see. Uranus has more than ten faint rings around it. Even with powerful telescopes, nobody saw these rings until 1977. Then, when the space probe Voyager 2 passed by Uranus in 1986, scientists found more rings.

Why are the rings so hard to see? First, the rings are made mostly out of dust. Dust does not reflect light very well. Second, Uranus is very far away. It is twice as far from the sun as Saturn is. Very little sunlight reaches Uranus.

Uranus was discovered about two hundred years ago by William Herschel. He used a telescope to keep watch on a faint object in the dark sky. The object did not act like a star. Unlike a star, which would appear to be fixed in the sky, Uranus shifted its position a tiny bit. The object seemed to move through the stars. It turned out to be a planet, Uranus.

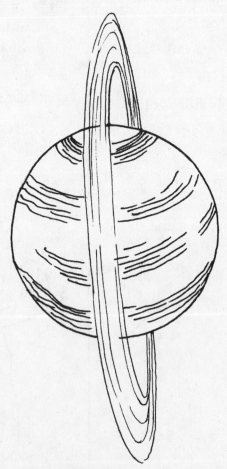

---

1 The rings of Uranus were first seen—

Ⓐ near Saturn

Ⓑ in 1977

Ⓒ in 1986

Ⓓ by William Herschel

2 To find out about other planets, you should—

Ⓕ look at the night sky

Ⓖ buy a microscope

Ⓗ visit an art museum

Ⓙ look in an encyclopedia

3 Why did William Herschel think the object he saw was not a star?

Ⓐ It had rings.

Ⓑ It was green.

Ⓒ It changed its position.

Ⓓ It was dim and dusty.

4 This story would probably be found in a book about—

Ⓕ our solar system

Ⓖ the earth's oceans

Ⓗ going to the moon

Ⓙ how globes are made

5 The seventh planet from the sun is—

Ⓐ Uranus

Ⓑ Saturn

Ⓒ Voyager

Ⓓ Earth

6 Why does little sunlight reach Uranus?

Ⓕ It is made of dust.

Ⓖ It is far from the sun.

Ⓗ It has rings that block the light.

Ⓙ It moves through the stars.

Rita Goes Skiing

Rita was going skiing with her mom today. She had never skied before. Rita's mother loved skiing. She never fell when she went down the mountain. Rita wanted to be a good skiier, too. She hoped to go down the mountain without falling.

Rita was a little scared, though. She was afraid that skiing would be hard. Even though Rita was wearing a helmet, she still feared that she might hurt herself.

Her mother told her not to worry. She told Rita that the helmet would keep her safe and that she wouldn't leave her side. She promised that they would go slowly down the hill.

They took a "rope tow" up the hill. Rita's mom showed her how to hold on tight and to let the rope pull her up the hill. They reached the top and let go of the rope. Rita's mom stayed by her side and helped her ski down the hill for the first time. Even though they went slowly, Rita fell. It didn't hurt at all. Rita just dug her poles in the ground, lifted herself up, and tried again. The next time she went down the hill, she fell again. She got up with no trouble, though, and dusted herself off. The third time Rita didn't fall at all. She wasn't scared anymore. She really liked skiing.

At the end of the day, Rita was skiing very well. She didn't even want to stop. She thanked her mom for taking her skiing. She couldn't wait to go again.

7 What could this passage also be titled?

   Ⓐ "Rita's Hobbies"

   Ⓑ "Falling Down"

   © "Not Afraid Anymore"

   Ⓓ "How to Ski"

8 The passage gives you enough information to know that—

   Ⓕ Rita is very young.

   Ⓖ Rita's mother is a good skiier.

   Ⓗ Rita likes a lot of sports.

   Ⓙ Rita is a good student.

9 Before Rita went skiing, she hoped that she would <u>not</u>—

   Ⓐ be cold

   Ⓑ like skiing

   © go again sometime

   Ⓓ fall down

10 What do you think will happen the next time Rita goes skiing?

   Ⓕ She won't be afraid.

   Ⓖ She will not fall.

   Ⓗ She will go alone.

   Ⓙ She won't ever go again.

11 What did Rita's mother promise?

   Ⓐ To catch Rita when she fell

   Ⓑ To go slowly down the hill

   © To buy her new skis

   Ⓓ To go fast down the hill

STOP

Directions

Read each passage and answer the questions that follow.

Mesas and Cliff Dwellings

Mesas are gigantic rocks that have steep cliffs and flat tops. The word mesa means "table" in Spanish. Mesas are common in the southwest United States.

Hundreds of years ago, people lived in the rock walls of some mesas. They actually carved small towns into the sides of the rock cliffs. Because the cliffs were hard to climb the people who lived there were safe from their enemies. The people who built these towns were <u>ancestors</u> of modern day Pueblo people. Some parts of these towns, known as cliff dwellings, are still standing today.

Cliff Palace is the name of one of these places in Colorado. It contains more than two hundred rooms. Cliff Palace was built into the side of Mesa Verde, a huge mesa with a forest growing on top of it. The people who lived in Cliff Palace were farmers. They planted crops in the valley below the mesa.

There are other old town sites on Mesa Verde. Some are cliff dwellings, like Cliff Palace. Others are found on top of the mesa. You can see these places if you visit Mesa Verde National Park.

1 Mesas are made of—

Ⓐ wood

Ⓑ rock

Ⓒ forests

Ⓓ dwellings

2 The writer feels that Cliff Palace is—

Ⓕ fit for a king

Ⓖ a poor place to hide

Ⓗ a fantasy

Ⓙ a good place to visit

3 In this story, the <u>ancestors</u> are—

Ⓐ relatives of Pueblo people

Ⓑ scientists from Colorado

Ⓒ park rangers

Ⓓ southwestern cowboys

4 What should the reader do to answer question 3?

Ⓕ Read the name of the story a second time.

Ⓖ Read the first sentence of the story again.

Ⓗ Look in the first paragraph of the story.

Ⓙ Look for the word <u>ancestors</u> in the story.

5 What is another good name for the story?

Ⓐ "Old Towns of Mesa Verde"

Ⓑ "Colorado Farmers"

Ⓒ "Forest on the Mesa"

Ⓓ "Rock Climbing in the Southwest"

6 This story was written to—

Ⓕ teach about a job

Ⓖ give a list of rules

Ⓗ tell about a place

Ⓙ show how to fix something

Giving Your Turtle A Check-up

You can tell if your turtle is healthy by watching it. Check to see that your turtle moves around sometimes. Remember that some kinds of turtles move around in the evening rather than in the daytime. All turtles should walk evenly. They should not walk with one side down. They should not walk with a back leg dragging.

You can also tell how your turtle is doing when you feed it. A healthy turtle likes its food. It will not refuse food.

Examine your turtle every week or so. Giving your turtle a check-up can be fun. It can also help you get to know your turtle better.

1.   Pick up your turtle. Gently and carefully press on the back and belly. Unless your turtle is very young, its shell should be hard.

2.   Look in the folds of the skin. The skin should not have any cuts.

3.   Look at your turtle's eyes. They should be open and clear.

4.   Look at the nostrils and mouth. There should be no bubbles.

5.   Listen to your turtle breathe. It should breathe quietly.

7 The final step in the check-up is to—

Ⓐ look at the turtle's eyes

Ⓑ look at the nostrils and mouth

Ⓒ pick up the turtle and press on the back and belly

Ⓓ listen to the turtle breathe

8 Why do you press on the back and belly?

Ⓕ To see how heavy the turtle is

Ⓖ To check the turtle's breathing

Ⓗ To make sure that its shell is hard

Ⓙ To check the turtle's hind legs

9 During which part of the check-up is it probably most important to be very quiet?

Ⓐ When you look at the turtle's eyes

Ⓑ When you feed the turtle

Ⓒ When you watch the turtle walk

Ⓓ When you listen to the turtle breathe

10 You would probably find this flyer—

Ⓕ in a pet shop

Ⓖ at a circus

Ⓗ in a music store

Ⓙ at the library

11 Another good title for this flyer is—

Ⓐ "Turtles, Toads, and Lizards"

Ⓑ "Feeding Your Turtle"

Ⓒ "How to Tell if Your Turtle is Healthy"

Ⓓ "Building a House for a Turtle"

12 How often should you examine your turtle?

Ⓕ Every month or so

Ⓖ Every week or so

Ⓗ Every other day

Ⓙ Every day

STOP

Directions

Read each passage and answer the questions that follow.

Chris and the Old Barn

For as long as Chris could remember, the barn across the street had been empty. The red paint was peeling off the side and the doors sagged open. No one ever went there. No animals lived inside.

Chris's friends thought the barn was scary and a mess. Chris liked the old barn, though. He looked at it every night from his bedroom window. He felt sorry that no one cared about the barn. He wished someone would take care of it.

"I wish that barn would get fixed. I wish it would be the most cheerful barn anyone has ever seen, with lots of animals living inside," Chris thought before he slid into bed.

When Chris woke up the next morning, he heard a loud noise coming from outside. He jumped out of bed and ran to the window to look. *Vrooooom! Va-vroooom!* Chris saw a large red truck drive past his house and stop in front of the barn. He watched as five people climbed out of the truck. All of them were wearing jeans and T-shirts with words written on them. They all carried toolboxes. They opened the barn's doors and walked inside.

Soon Chris heard noises from inside the barn. He heard the bang of a hammer. He heard the hum of an electric drill. "What are they doing?" wondered Chris. At that moment, a second truck drove down the street. It pulled in next to the red truck and stopped. Four people got out of the truck. They unloaded ladders, buckets of paint, and paint brushes.

Chris leaned out the window and shouted to the people below, "Are you painting that old barn?"

One of them heard Chris and answered him. "That's right. We're going to turn it into the most cheerful barn anyone has ever seen." The *most cheerful barn* . . . Chris remembered what he had wished for the night before. His eyes were wide with surprise. His wish had come true!

1 Chris wanted—

   Ⓐ the barn to be taken care of

   Ⓑ the people in the truck to visit him

   Ⓒ the neighbors to visit the barn

   Ⓓ the animals in the barn to be quiet

2 Who were the people in the truck?

   Ⓕ Cowboys

   Ⓖ Workers

   Ⓗ Chris's classmates

   Ⓙ Chris's family

3 The sound that woke Chris was from —

   Ⓐ a lawn mower

   Ⓑ a rooster

   Ⓒ his alarm clock

   Ⓓ a truck

Handy Dandy

Here is a game you can play with your friends.

Materials:

Any small object that can fit in your hand

How to play:

1. Place the object in either hand.

2. Place your hands behind your back. You may choose to keep the object in the same hand that you put it in or you may want to switch it into your other hand. The point is to confuse the player who will guess which hand the object is in.

3. Put your hands in front you, one on top of the other.

4. Sing this song:

    Handy Dandy riddly row
    Which do you pick the high or the low?

5. While you are singing move your hands one on top of the other until the song ends.

6. When the song ends, the other players must guess if the object is in the hand on top or the hand on the bottom.

7. The person who guesses correctly becomes the leader and gets to hide the object next.

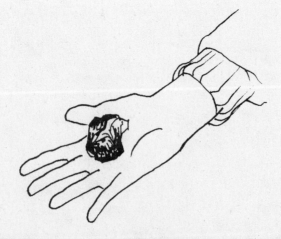

4 How many people does this game require?

Ⓐ One

Ⓑ Two

Ⓒ Three

Ⓓ The story does not say.

5 In which step does the object first go in your hand?

Ⓕ One

Ⓖ Two

Ⓗ Three

Ⓙ Four

6 The purpose of the song is to—

Ⓐ make everyone who is playing dance

Ⓑ make the game more fun

Ⓒ explain the rules

Ⓓ guess where the object is

7 How would the game become unfair?

Ⓕ If you can not guess

Ⓖ If the object was too big to fit in the player's hand

Ⓗ If the song is sung out of tune

Ⓙ If it is played at night

8 How does someone become the next leader?

Ⓐ If you guess correctly.

Ⓑ If you are the most intelligent in the group.

Ⓒ When all the other players have given up.

Ⓓ When all the players have given voted.

9 You would most likely find this game in a book called—

Ⓕ *Winter Activities*

Ⓖ *Kids' Sports*

Ⓗ *Fun Games for Us*

Ⓙ *Fill in the Blanks*

Directions

Read each passage and answer the questions that follow.

A Man and His Ox

Long ago a farmer walked to town with his ox, Sweet Friend.

"In the past I fed you well, Sweet Friend," the man said to his ox. "Now our crops have failed. We must buy some food, but I have little money."

"Sir, you have treated me with great care," replied the ox. "You have fed me well. I am the strongest ox in the valley. Why not brag to a merchant that I can pull a sled of stones?" suggested Sweet Friend.

"What a good idea, my great ox," said the man.

When they got to town, the man told a merchant that his ox could pull a sled of stones.

"No single ox can do that," said the merchant. "Show me, old man. If your ox succeeds, I will give you ten bags of rice."

The man hooked a sled of stones to Sweet Friend's harness. "Let's go, you beast! Come on, you scamp, move!" cried the man.

Sweet Friend could hardly believe his ears. "I am not a scamp," thought the ox. "Why does he shout so?"

Sweet Friend refused to move. The merchant laughed. The man unhooked his ox. They walked back home in silence.

The next morning, Sweet Friend said to the man, "Sir, I have always done my best for you. But yesterday you treated me harshly. The thought of free rice made you forget about kindness."

"You're right, Sweet Friend. I am sorry."

"Let's try again today," said the ox.

They walked back to town. Sure enough, the merchant made the same offer.

The man gently hooked the sled to the harness. "Okay, Sweet Friend. Ready to go, my great ox." Sweet Friend moved his thick legs and pulled the sled all the way down the street.

"Thank you, Sweet Friend," said the man as he hugged the ox. "We now have enough rice for winter."

---

1 The man and his ox walked to town to—

Ⓐ sell hay

Ⓑ buy food

Ⓒ watch a circus

Ⓒ grow crops

2 The merchant probably thought the man was—

Ⓕ foolish

Ⓖ handsome

Ⓗ young

Ⓘ rich

3 What lesson does this story teach?

Ⓐ Never brag to a stranger.

Ⓑ It's best to tell the truth.

Ⓒ A man and an ox make good friends.

Ⓓ Kindness always matters.

4 How can you tell that this story is make-believe?

Ⓕ A farmer's crops cannot fail.

Ⓖ An ox cannot talk.

Ⓗ A merchant cannot give away rice.

Ⓘ A man cannot shout at an ox.

5 When the story ends, Sweet Friend most likely feels—

Ⓐ interested

Ⓑ afraid

Ⓒ joyful

Ⓓ sad

6 The writer tells the story to show—

Ⓕ how the farmer and the ox got their winter rice

Ⓖ why the farmer and the ox went separate ways

Ⓗ how the farmer named his ox

Ⓘ why an ox is always stubborn

Alphabet Memory Game

Here is a game to play when you do not have any toys or supplies with you. You do not need any materials. You just need a good memory. You can play with at least three players, but the more players, the better.

The youngest player starts. The next youngest is second. And so on.

How to play:

1   The first player says the name of something that begins with the letter A. The word can be anything, such as an animal, a kind of fruit, or a tool that you use around the house. It can even be something imaginary.

2   The second player must repeat the first player's word. Then the second player says the name of something that begins with the letter B.

3   The third player repeats the first two words in the correct order. Then the third player adds the name of something that begins with the letter C.

4   As the game goes on, the list of words is said out loud during each player's turn. Everyone takes turns until someone forgets one of the words in the list. The player who forgets the word is out. The rest keep on playing.

5   The last player left wins. If you make it to the end of the alphabet, everyone who is left playing wins. You can leave off the last three letters of the alphabet, X, Y, and Z, to make things simpler.

An example of how to play:

Player 1 says *apple*

Player 2 says *apple, bear*

Player 3 says *apple, bear, candle*

Player 1 says *apple, bear, candle, dragon*

Player 2 says *apple, bear, candle, dragon, earlobe*

7 The first thing you must do on your turn is to—

  Ⓐ say the name of an animal

  Ⓑ say the name of something that begins with the next letter

  Ⓒ repeat the list of words

  Ⓓ repeat the alphabet

8 You would probably find this game in a book with the title—

  Ⓕ *Activities that Make You Think*

  Ⓖ *Games to Play with Music*

  Ⓗ *Painting by Letters*

  Ⓙ *Underwater Alphabet*

9 Who goes first in this game?

  Ⓐ The tallest player

  Ⓑ The youngest player

  Ⓒ The player without any materials

  Ⓓ The first player to say *apple*

10 It would be unfair if one of the players—

  Ⓕ secretly wrote down the list of words

  Ⓖ forgot the first word on the list

  Ⓗ forgot the last word on the list

  Ⓙ used the name of a vegetable as a new word

11 If you forget a word while repeating the list, you—

  Ⓐ are allowed to ask a younger player to help

  Ⓑ lose a point

  Ⓒ say two new words instead of just one

  Ⓓ are out of the game

12 The player who wins is probably good at—

  Ⓕ drawing cartoons

  Ⓖ adding big numbers

  Ⓗ remembering things

  Ⓙ singing songs

STOP

Directions

Read each passage and answer the questions that follow.

Do You Want to Go to Day Camp?

Last July, Trisha's mother told her she wanted Trisha to go to day camp for a week. Her mother said that the camp was outside the city. It had woods, meadows, and a lake to swim in. It had an art room where kids could make drawings and crafts.

Trisha did not want to go. She wanted to stay and play with her neighborhood friends. Trisha tried to explain, but her mother would not change her mind. She said that she thought Trisha would really like the camp. She asked Trisha to try it for at least one day. Trisha agreed, but she was not very happy.

The next morning, Trisha was on a bus with nine other children who she did not know. She sulked the whole way to Camp Silver Hill. When she got off the bus, Trisha noticed the fresh scent of pine trees. She saw a rabbit scurry into the woods. She looked down at a wide lake. "This camp is very pretty," she thought to herself.

Ms. Tina, the head counselor, greeted Trisha's group. She told them a little about the camp. She said the first thing they would do was to take a swim test. Then they would paddle a canoe across the lake.

Trisha grinned. She had never paddled a canoe before! She was so excited about the canoe trip that she forgot to be grumpy. Trisha passed her swim test. Then she got ready for the canoe trip.

Trisha put on her life jacket. An adult balanced the canoe as Trisha climbed into its front end. Then Ms. Tina got in. Before she knew it, Trisha was paddling the canoe across the lake while Ms. Tina steered from the back. "This is great," thought Trisha. "I sure am glad Mom convinced me to come."

1 Trisha went to the camp during which season?

Ⓐ Winter

Ⓑ Spring

Ⓒ Summer

Ⓓ Fall

2 As Trisha got off the bus, she noticed—

Ⓕ the art room

Ⓖ the scent of pine trees

Ⓗ several canoes beside the bus

Ⓚ the sound of a river

3 When Trisha learned they were going to paddle canoes, she felt—

Ⓐ happy and enthusiastic

Ⓑ sick to her stomach

Ⓒ bored and grumpy

Ⓓ like she should just watch

4 Trisha saw a rabbit that—

Ⓕ wiggled its nose

Ⓖ nibbled a leaf

Ⓗ froze in fear

Ⓚ hopped away

Greenville Sports Association
Soccer Program

Dear Soccer Players and Parents,

We had a great season this fall! To celebrate our success, we are having roller-skating parties at Skate Palace.

For players in the "up to six-year-old" and "up to eight-year-old" leagues, we will have a party on Monday, November 22, from 6:00 to 8:30.

For players in the "up to ten-year-old" and "up to twelve-year -old" leagues, we will have a party on Sunday, November 28, from 3:00 to 5:30.

The cost for each party is $1 per person. The cost includes skate rental. Players, parents, and other family members are invited.

We ask that all soccer players and parents do the following:

1) wash their uniforms.
2) clean any other equipment they have borrowed.
3) turn in their uniforms and equipment to their coaches by Saturday, November 20. (Coaches must return everything to the league office by Sunday, November 21.)

Please remember that the Greenville Sports Association also offers programs in basketball, softball, and flag football.

Best wishes,

Mrs. Asad

Mrs. Asad
President of the Soccer Program

5 A seven-year-old soccer player should go to Skate Palace on—

(A) November 20

(B) November 21

(C) November 22

(D) November 28

6 Uniforms must be turned in—

(F) before the skating parties

(G) at the first skating party

(H) at the second skating party

(J) after the skating parties

7 Where did soccer players probably receive these letters?

(A) At school

(B) At their first soccer practice of the season

(C) At their homes

(D) At a sporting goods store

8 Which sport is <u>not</u> talked about in the letter?

(F) Basketball

(G) Hockey

(H) Flag football

(J) Softball

9 Before you turn in your uniform, you should—

(A) pay for the skating party

(B) find out whether or not to keep it for next year

(C) wash it

(D) put your name on it

10 What time does the party on Sunday, November 28, begin?

(F) Three o'clock

(G) Four o'clock

(H) Five o'clock

(J) Six o'clock

STOP

Directions

Read each passage and answer the questions that follow.

The Fountain

Every day Kevin and Tara walked by the park and waved to the dolphins. These weren't real dolphins, they were statues of two dolphins leaping into the air from a pool of water. Their pool was empty though, and the fountains were off. The dolphins were chipped and covered with green moss. Kevin and Tara's mother told them that when she was young, the dolphins were bright and shiny. The pool was full and lights lit the fountain at night. The water had sparkled as it leapt through the air.

"People used to throw coins in the fountain and make wishes," Mom said.

"I'd wish that the fountains were back on, and the dolphins were new and shiny again," Tara sighed.

"Hey! Maybe we should make a wish!" said Kevin.

Tara searched her pockets. "I don't have any coins," she said.

That day, Kevin and Tara returned to the fountain with a couple of pennies. They threw their coins into the dry pool. They both closed their eyes and made wishes.

The next morning, Kevin and Tara raced to the park to check out the statues. Everything was the same. Tara thought the dolphins looked sadder than ever.

Then, a week later, as Tara and Kevin walked by one bright sunny morning, they saw a group of people carrying buckets and scrub brushes.

"Where are you going?" asked Tara. The people explained that they were going to the old fountain. They were going to spend the day cleaning the fountain and its dolphins for free.

"Our wishes *did* come true!" said Kevin.

1 Tara hoped that —

Ⓐ she could swim in the fountain

Ⓑ the dolphins were real

Ⓒ the fountain would be cleaned

Ⓓ Kevin would be quiet

2 Why were Tara and Kevin sad about the fountain?

Ⓓ It had become old and dirty.

Ⓔ Their mother didn't like it.

Ⓘ They didn't have any coins to throw into it.

Ⓚ The dolphins weren't real.

3 Who were the people with the buckets?

Ⓐ Park rangers

Ⓑ Students

Ⓒ People doing a good deed

Ⓓ Paid workers

4 What is likely to happen next?

Ⓓ The fountain will be taken away.

Ⓔ Kevin and Tara will give the people money.

Ⓘ The people will clean the fountain.

Ⓚ Park rangers will ask the group to leave.

Growing Sunflowers

Sunflowers are fun to grow because the plants get tall very fast. Once the sunflowers are dry, the seeds from the middle of the bright flowers make great bird food.

What you need:

a packet of sunflower seeds from a store
an outdoor garden spot that gets a lot of sun
plenty of water
an adult helper

When to start:

Wait until early summer. Sunflowers do best in hot weather.

What to do:

1. Get an adult to prepare the garden spot. Your adult helper may need to add some <u>fertilizer</u> to the soil. It will give the sunflower plants extra food.

2. Make a little hole in the soil. It should be about a half an inch deep. Drop in a seed. Cover the seed with soil. Plant them about a foot and a half apart. Plant as many seeds as you wish.

3. Water the seeds.

4. Keep the soil moist. Soon the seeds will sprout. You will probably need to water the plants almost every day.

5. Watch your sunflowers reach for the sky!

5 Why should you plant the seeds after summer begins?

  Ⓐ It will be easier to take care of the plants.

  Ⓑ It rains too much in the spring.

  Ⓒ The plant grows best when the weather is hot.

  Ⓓ The plants are hard to see in the snow.

6 In which step do the directions say that you need an adult's help?

  Ⓕ Step 1

  Ⓖ Step 2

  Ⓗ Step 3

  Ⓙ Step 4

7 In step 1, the word <u>fertilizer</u> means—

  Ⓐ beach sand

  Ⓑ cold water

  Ⓒ plant food

  Ⓓ insect spray

8 Where would you most likely find these instructions?

  Ⓕ In a cookbook

  Ⓖ In a music book

  Ⓗ On a poster in a grocery store

  Ⓙ In a gardening book

9 How deep should you plant the seeds?

  Ⓐ About a half a foot

  Ⓑ About half an inch

  Ⓑ About a foot

  Ⓒ One yard

10 Where should you plant the seeds?

  Ⓕ In the shade

  Ⓖ In a sunny spot

  Ⓗ Indoors

  Ⓙ Under a tree

STOP

Reading Vocabulary

DIRECTIONS

Read the sample sentence inside the box. Then choose the answer that uses the underlined word in the same way as it is used in the example.

SAMPLE A

 A   You can <u>slip</u> and fall on an icy sidewalk.

Which answer uses the word <u>slip</u> the same way as it is above?

ⓐ The cat tried to <u>slip</u> between the two fences.

ⓑ The bride wore a <u>slip</u> under her gown.

ⓒ Please write your name on this <u>slip</u> of paper.

ⓓ I was afraid I would <u>slip</u> on the wet floor.

1   The newspaper article was <u>clear</u>.

Which answer uses the word <u>clear</u> in the same way as it is above?

ⓐ Maybe the police office can <u>clear</u> up this mess.

ⓑ The boat left the harbor and made it into the <u>clear</u>.

ⓒ Tanya's explanation is <u>clear</u> to me.

ⓓ The sky started to <u>clear</u> after the rain stopped.

 2   Please be careful not to <u>break</u> the glass.

Which answer uses the word <u>break</u> the same way as it is above?

ⓕ Can we take a <u>break</u> from walking?

ⓖ If you fall you may <u>break</u> your arm.

ⓗ You should never <u>break</u> the law.

ⓙ The farmer was tired so he took a <u>break</u>.

 3   Suzie's brother calls her a little <u>kid</u>.

Which answer uses the word <u>kid</u> the same way as it is above?

ⓐ A baby goat is called a <u>kid</u>.

ⓑ My big brother likes to tell jokes and <u>kid</u> around.

ⓒ That park is where I played when I was a <u>kid</u>.

ⓓ It is fun to <u>kid</u> people on April Fool's Day.

 4   Do not <u>drop</u> the dish.

Which answer uses the word <u>drop</u> the same way as it is above?

ⓕ Can we <u>drop</u> in and see Uncle John?

ⓖ I had to <u>drop</u> the match because it was hot.

ⓗ A <u>drop</u> of soda spilled on the rug.

ⓙ Did I just see a shoe <u>drop</u>?

DIRECTIONS

Look at the underlined word in each question. Then, choose the answer that is closest in meaning to the underlined word.

SAMPLE B

B A <u>sack</u> is a kind of—

- Ⓐ dance
- Ⓑ bag*
- Ⓒ weight
- Ⓓ show

5 A <u>rag</u> is a—

- Ⓐ post
- Ⓑ fence
- Ⓒ broom
- Ⓓ cloth

6 To <u>manage</u> is to—

- Ⓕ work
- Ⓖ wait
- Ⓗ shop
- Ⓙ control

7 A <u>strategy</u> is a—

- Ⓐ plan
- Ⓑ battle
- Ⓒ game
- Ⓓ enemy

8 A <u>model</u> is a(n)—

- Ⓕ book
- Ⓖ plane
- Ⓗ show
- Ⓙ example

9 Something that is <u>injured</u> is—

- Ⓐ hard
- Ⓑ fair
- Ⓒ shy
- Ⓓ hurt

10 Something <u>valuable</u> is—

- Ⓕ interesting
- Ⓖ worthwhile
- Ⓗ shiny
- Ⓙ complete

11 <u>Tardy</u> means—

- Ⓐ late
- Ⓑ busy
- Ⓒ sick
- Ⓓ strict

12 To <u>shelter</u> is to—

- Ⓕ give
- Ⓖ protect
- Ⓗ build
- Ⓙ camp

13 When you are <u>astonished</u>, you are—

- Ⓐ joyful
- Ⓑ frightened
- Ⓒ polite
- Ⓓ amazed

14 To be <u>crafty</u> is to be—

Ⓐ sly

Ⓑ wicked

Ⓒ talented

Ⓓ lazy

15 Something that is <u>flawless</u> is—

Ⓕ shiny

Ⓖ wide

Ⓗ perfect

Ⓙ tough

16 To <u>approve</u> is to—

Ⓐ draw

Ⓑ delay

Ⓒ accept

Ⓓ mark

17 If you <u>recall</u> something, you—

Ⓕ remember it

Ⓖ beat it

Ⓗ cut it

Ⓙ toss it

18 <u>Camouflage</u> means—

Ⓐ to divide

Ⓑ to decrease

Ⓒ to disguise

Ⓓ to abandon

19 A <u>stack</u> is a—

Ⓕ house

Ⓖ puppy

Ⓗ pile

Ⓙ river

20 <u>Lovely</u> means—

Ⓐ dry

Ⓑ fake

Ⓒ easy

Ⓓ pretty

21 Something <u>grimy</u> is—

Ⓕ dirty

Ⓖ slow

Ⓗ quiet

Ⓙ happy

22 Something that is <u>blaring</u> is—

Ⓐ helpful

Ⓑ noisy

Ⓒ walking

Ⓓ sitting

23 To <u>tend</u> is to—

Ⓕ care for

Ⓖ hold onto

Ⓗ look for

Ⓙ pass by

DIRECTIONS

Use the words in the sentence to help you figure out the meaning of the underlined word. Then mark the space for your answer choice.

SAMPLE C

C The actors had to <u>rehearse</u> their lines over and over to prepare for the actual performance. **<u>Rehearse</u> means –**

Ⓐ sing

Ⓑ write

Ⓒ repeat

Ⓓ study

24 The tall fence will <u>obstruct</u> my view of your backyard. **<u>Obstruct</u> means—**

Ⓕ block

Ⓖ fix

Ⓗ improve

Ⓙ rot

25 The lost puppy seemed <u>content</u> after we gave it a bath and some food. **<u>Content</u> means—**

Ⓐ angry

Ⓑ happy

Ⓒ nervous

Ⓓ sad

26 My cat is very <u>plump</u>, even though it does not eat much food. **<u>Plump</u> means—**

Ⓕ thirsty

Ⓖ soft

Ⓗ chubby

Ⓙ sleepy

27 My grandmother never told a lie and was always <u>sincere</u>. **<u>Sincere</u> means—**

Ⓐ sneaky

Ⓑ unhappy

Ⓒ smiling

Ⓓ honest

28 Since Gabriel forgot to water the flower, it began to <u>droop</u>. **<u>Droop</u> means—**

Ⓕ hang down

Ⓖ soften

Ⓗ blossom

Ⓙ grow

29 Since there is a <u>shortage</u> of water, we can only take one bath a week. **<u>Shortage</u> means—**

Ⓐ barrel

Ⓑ supply

Ⓒ lack

Ⓓ large amount

30 Anna looked <u>hideous</u> when she dressed up as an old witch with green make-up. **<u>Hideous</u> means—**

Ⓕ ugly

Ⓖ happy

Ⓗ beautiful

Ⓙ thin

31 The mouse <u>darted</u> into its hole when it saw the cat. **<u>Darted</u> means—**

Ⓐ bit

Ⓑ squeaked

Ⓒ walked slowly

Ⓓ moved quickly

STOP

DIRECTIONS

Use the words in the sentence to help you figure out the meaning of the underlined word. Then mark the space for your answer choice.

SAMPLE A

A I <u>exchanged</u> one pair of shoes for another I liked better. <u>Exchanged</u> means—

Ⓐ lent

Ⓑ stretched

Ⓒ traded

Ⓓ squeezed

1 It is <u>risky</u> to skate on thin ice since you may fall through. <u>Risky</u> means—

Ⓐ dangerous

Ⓑ helpful

Ⓒ amusing

Ⓓ clover

2 He gave his <u>reply</u> almost before she could finish asking her question. <u>Reply</u> means—

Ⓐ shift

Ⓑ speech

Ⓒ answer

Ⓓ cup

3 They <u>snipped</u> and trimmed until the cloth was the right size. <u>Snipped</u> means—

Ⓐ saved

Ⓑ cut

Ⓒ painted

Ⓓ swept

4 She <u>reserved</u> her seat by asking a friend to hold her place. <u>Reserved</u> means—

Ⓐ kept

Ⓑ stood

Ⓒ melted

Ⓓ traded

5 The <u>purpose</u> for the class was to learn to read. <u>Purpose</u> means—

Ⓐ belt

Ⓑ advertisement

Ⓒ reason

Ⓓ seed

6 He had no doubts, and was <u>certain</u> they would win. <u>Certain</u> means—

Ⓐ well

Ⓑ pulled

Ⓒ sure

Ⓓ careful

7 He was <u>timid</u>, and felt nervous in big crowds. <u>Timid</u> means—

Ⓐ fast

Ⓑ shy

Ⓒ poor

Ⓓ rocky

8 The microscope helped <u>magnify</u> the tiny germ, and made it large enough to see. <u>Magnify</u> means—

Ⓐ press

Ⓑ make larger

Ⓒ make smoother

Ⓓ make lower

9 There was only one <u>particular</u> size that would fit, and only one store carried it. <u>Particular</u> means—

Ⓐ pretty

Ⓐ soft

Ⓒ certain

Ⓓ very

10 He <u>stumbled</u> clumsily on the steps and landed on the carpet. <u>Stumbled</u> means—

Ⓕ flipped

Ⓖ swelled

Ⓗ tripped

Ⓙ left

11 She <u>carved</u> the large loaf of bread into sixteen slices. <u>Carved</u> means—

Ⓐ buttered

Ⓑ frosted

Ⓒ brewed

Ⓓ sliced

12 He <u>recalled</u> a story from long ago, when he was a very young boy. <u>Recalled</u> means—

Ⓕ remembered

Ⓖ told

Ⓗ marked

Ⓙ peeled

13 We <u>anticipated</u> that we would arrive in three hours. <u>Anticipated</u> means—

Ⓐ brought

Ⓑ wrote

Ⓒ expected

Ⓓ called

14 We decided to use <u>artificial</u> flowers, because they would last longer than real ones. <u>Artificial</u> means—

Ⓕ fake

Ⓖ next

Ⓗ striped

Ⓙ softer

15 We believe that we are <u>capable</u> of winning a championship because all of our players are so good. <u>Capable</u> means—

Ⓐ toward

Ⓑ laboring

Ⓒ able

Ⓓ wrong

16 The <u>brutal</u>, terrible cold sent us shivering back to our homes. <u>Brutal</u> means—

Ⓕ light

Ⓖ icy

Ⓗ chunky

Ⓙ harsh

17 We <u>combined</u> our money to see if that would add up to enough for the present. <u>Combined</u> means—

Ⓐ put together

Ⓑ alphabetized

Ⓒ set down

Ⓓ ruled out

18 We were <u>baffled</u> by the mystery and could not find the answer. <u>Baffled</u> means—

Ⓕ puzzled

Ⓖ relieved

Ⓗ reminded

Ⓙ posted

DIRECTIONS

Look at the underlined word in each question. Then, choose the answer that is closest in meaning to the underlined word.

SAMPLE B

B To <u>repair</u> means to—

Ⓐ do again

Ⓐ notice

Ⓒ destroy

Ⓓ fix

19 An <u>award</u> is a—

Ⓐ place

Ⓑ prize

Ⓒ cow

Ⓓ sink

20 A <u>goal</u> is a(n)—

Ⓕ aim

Ⓖ example

Ⓗ trade

Ⓙ heavy

21 To <u>shiver</u> is to—

Ⓐ mend

Ⓑ bowl

Ⓒ shake

Ⓓ bend

22 A <u>tale</u> is a—

Ⓕ story

Ⓖ bone

Ⓗ step

Ⓙ gun

23 A <u>cushion</u> is a kind of—

Ⓐ window

Ⓑ pillow

Ⓒ shirt

Ⓓ desk

24 Something that is <u>equal</u> is the—

Ⓕ best

Ⓖ same

Ⓗ only

Ⓙ last

25 To <u>invent</u> is to—

Ⓐ create

Ⓑ own

Ⓒ color

Ⓓ dry

26 <u>Stack</u> means—

Ⓕ house

Ⓖ puppy

Ⓗ pile

Ⓙ river

27 To <u>chatter</u> is to—

Ⓐ help

Ⓑ run

Ⓒ cry

Ⓓ talk

DIRECTIONS

Read the sample sentence inside the box. Then choose the answer that uses the underlined word in the same way as it is used in the example.

SAMPLE C

> Look at the ball roll down the hill!

Which answer uses the word roll in the same way as it is above?

Ⓐ Where is the roll of paper towels?

Ⓑ My aunt gave me a roll of quarters

Ⓒ James can roll a coin across the room.

Ⓓ The teacher took roll call to see who was missing.

> I may be late tomorrow.

Which answer uses the word may in the same way as it is above?

Ⓕ May is the best month of the year.

Ⓖ It may be hard for us to carry that box.

Ⓗ May I please have a candy bar?

Ⓙ You may have one cookie before dinner.

> Our cabin is at the foot of the mountain.

Which answer uses the word foot in the same way as it is above?

Ⓐ My lizard is a foot long.

Ⓑ The mouse dug a nest at the foot of the tree.

Ⓒ My foot really hurts.

Ⓓ He missed the basket by one foot.

> Look at that band of singers.

Which answer uses the word band in the same way as it is above?

Ⓕ We must all band together if we want to win.

Ⓖ I belong to a band of actors.

Ⓗ He is wearing a band on his wrist.

Ⓙ Is that a rubber band?

> How do I tie this knot?

Which answer uses the word tie in the same way as it is above?

Ⓐ My father wears a tie every day.

Ⓑ The hockey game ended in a tie score.

Ⓒ Little Peter can tie his own shoes now.

Ⓓ The last time they raced it was a tie.

> They had to open the hatch so we could enter the plane.

Which answer uses the word hatch in the same way as it is above?

Ⓕ The bank robbers were trying to hatch a plan.

Ⓖ A chicken sits on her eggs to hatch them.

Ⓗ A door on a submarine is called a hatch.

Ⓙ Fish eggs hatch under water.

Directions

Read each passage and answer the questions that follow.

Autumn Crafts Fair

Basket Weaving Demonstration

10:00–11:00 A.M. in the cafeteria

Mr. Elgin will show how to weave simple cane baskets.

Pumpkin Carving

Learn the best way to make a jack-o-lantern.

Come to the tent beside the playground. Bring your own pumpkin or buy one for $3.00.

12:00 noon–2:00 P.M.

Adult helpers are needed. Please talk to Marie Sanchez if you want to help.

Fourth Grade Music Concert

Songs for fall.

Ms. Erika Stone directs the fourth grade chorus group.

10:00–11:30 A.M. in Ms. Stone's room.

Corn Cob Dolls

2:00–3:00 P.M.

On the playground.

Louisa Ruiz will teach kids to make dolls and decorations out of squash and corn. There will be plenty of materials for everyone.

1 **Where should you go if you want to carve a pumpkin?**

Ⓐ The cafeteria

Ⓑ The tent beside the playground

Ⓒ Ms. Stone's room

Ⓓ On the playground

2 **Which craft is not found in the notices?**

Ⓕ Basket weaving

Ⓖ Pumpkin carving

Ⓗ Doll making

Ⓙ Birdhouse building

3 **Which activity will take place last?**

Ⓐ Mr. Elgin will show how to weave baskets.

Ⓑ Kids will learn how to make jack-o-lanterns.

Ⓒ Some of Ms. Stone's music students will give a concert.

Ⓓ Ms. Ruiz will show how to make things out of squash and corn.

4 **Who will run the basket weaving demonstration?**

Ⓕ Mr. Elgin

Ⓖ Ms. Stone

Ⓗ Ms. Ruiz

Ⓙ Ms. Sanchez

5 **You would probably find these notices—**

Ⓐ in a bus station

Ⓑ on an apartment building

Ⓒ at a swimming pool

Ⓓ at a school

6 **What time does the music concert start?**

Ⓕ 10:00 A.M.

Ⓖ 11:00 A.M.

Ⓗ 12:00 noon

Ⓙ 2:00 P.M.

A Trip to the Beach

Antonio rode in the backseat during the long drive. The last time he went to the beach, Antonio was just a small boy. Yet he still had memories of the wide blue sky, the gleaming sand, and the sound of calling sea gulls. Most of all, he remembered the huge surf. He used to run along the wet beach, watching the incoming waves.

Antonio looked out the side window. He made a promise to himself. This time he would actually go into the ocean. The car finally came to a stop. "We're here," his stepfather said.

Antonio brought along the same green bathing suit he used for swimming lessons. His mother had sewn a dolphin patch onto the trunks. The patch meant that Antonio had passed the swim class.

After changing, Antonio's family carried towels, an ice chest, and other supplies to the beach. His stepfather spread out a blanket on the warm sand. "Let's get to the water!" shouted Antonio.

He walked to the edge of ocean. He looked at the crashing waves. They were big, but not as big as he remembered. All of a sudden, his stepfather ran into the ocean and jumped over a passing wave. "Let's go, Antonio," said his stepfather loudly, waist deep in the water.

Antonio inched his way in until the water was up to his knees. A wave came splashing in, and knocked him down. Antonio, soaked from head to toe, jumped back to his feet. "That was fun," he said.

Antonio wiped his eyes and looked at the surf. He took a deep breath and bent down. Then he ran forward, jumped over a wave, and kept going. As the water got deeper, he began to paddle his arms. He reached his stepfather in no time.

Antonio stood up tall. The water was up to his chest. "These waves are great!" he cried.

7 Since his last beach trip, Antonio probably had become—

   Ⓐ afraid of water

   Ⓑ a better swimmer

   Ⓒ used to long car rides

   Ⓓ an expert in building sand castles

8 Who went into the ocean with Antonio?

   Ⓕ His stepfather

   Ⓖ His mother

   Ⓗ His swim coach

   Ⓙ His brother

9 What did Antonio remember most about his last trip to the beach?

   Ⓐ The sky

   Ⓑ The sand

   Ⓒ The sea gulls

   Ⓓ The surf

10 After Antonio got knocked down by a wave, he—

   Ⓕ wanted to get out and dry off

   Ⓖ became frightened

   Ⓗ remained determined to go in the ocean

   Ⓙ wished that the waves were bigger

11 What will most likely happen next in the story?

   Ⓐ It will start to rain.

   Ⓑ Antonio and his stepfather will play in the water.

   Ⓒ Antonio's mother will sew another patch on his trunks.

   Ⓓ Antonio and his stepfather will swim to a distant island.

STOP

Directions

Read each passage and answer the questions that follow.

Try this yummy popcorn recipe for a snack.

Here's what you need:

Cinnamon Popcorn

Popcorn (unpopped)
1/3 cup of butter
1/4 cup of packed brown sugar
1-1/2 teaspoons of cinnamon powder
A large bowl
A small bowl
A large paper bag

Ask an adult to help you make about three quarts of popped popcorn. Put the popcorn in a large bowl. Ask the adult to melt the butter and pour it over the popcorn.

In the small bowl, mix the brown sugar and cinnamon. Place the popcorn and the cinnamon-sugar mixture in a large paper bag. Close the bag tightly. Shake until the popcorn is evenly coated. Shaking the bag is fun! When you are finished, you will have about 12 cups of delicious cinnamon popcorn.

1 This snack could also be called—

Ⓐ Popcorn Balls

Ⓑ Cinnamon Cereal

Ⓒ Sweet Popcorn

Ⓓ Sour Popcorn

2 The second step is to—

Ⓕ close the bag

Ⓖ melt the butter

Ⓗ pop the popcorn

Ⓙ put the popcorn in a large bowl

3 You could find an idea like this by—

Ⓐ going to a drug store

Ⓑ looking in a cookbook

Ⓒ looking in a phonebook

Ⓓ going to a candy store

4 How much popcorn do you need to pop?

Ⓕ 1-1/2 teaspoons

Ⓖ 1/4 cup

Ⓗ 1/3 cup

Ⓙ 3 quarts

5 The small bowl is used for—

Ⓐ popping the popcorn

Ⓑ melting the butter

Ⓒ mixing the cinnamon and sugar

Ⓓ serving the cinnamon popcorn

Concentration

This is a fun game that two or more people can play.

You will need these items:

2 pieces of paper
a pen
a pair of scissors

Preparation:

1. Cut each piece of paper into 12 squares.
2. Draw a simple object on two squares of paper. Repeat this for all the squares. For example, a pair of smiley faces, a pair of apples, a pair of houses, etc.
3. Turn all of the squares face down. Arrange them in a 6 x 4 grid.

Rules:

1. The first person turns two of the squares face up. If they match, then that person keeps the squares. If they don't match, then they turn the squares face down again.
2. The second person takes their turn. If there are more players, then they each take a turn.
3. When all of the matching pairs are chosen, the winner is the player who has the most pairs.

6 How many squares of paper do you need to make?

- Ⓕ Two
- Ⓖ Six
- Ⓗ Twelve
- Ⓙ Twenty-four

7 You use the scissors for Preparation step —

- Ⓐ one
- Ⓑ two
- Ⓒ three
- Ⓓ You don't need the scissors for Preparation.

8 To find games like this, you would probably look in a book titled—

- Ⓕ *Riddles For Kids*
- Ⓖ *Games You Can Make Yourself*
- Ⓗ *Fun Computer Activities*
- Ⓙ *Wacky Word Games*

9 If you choose two matching objects, then—

- Ⓐ the next player loses a turn
- Ⓑ you get to keep the squares
- Ⓒ you leave them face up
- Ⓓ you turn them face down again

10 Each object is drawn onto two squares because—

- Ⓕ there are two pieces of paper
- Ⓖ you choose two squares in a turn
- Ⓗ this is a matching game
- Ⓙ there are at least two players

11 You should remember where the objects are because—

- Ⓐ there are so many objects
- Ⓑ it's a fast game
- Ⓒ the other players will choose the objects first
- Ⓓ it's easier to choose a match if you know where some of the objects are

STOP

Directions

Read each passage and answer the questions that follow.

Bronco Bertha

Cowboys are not the only heroes of the Wild West. There are some famous cowgirls too. One of the most famous cowgirls was Bertha Blanchett. She was known as the "greatest woman rider in the world." She competed in many rodeos. She rode broncos. A bronco is a wild horse.

In 1905, Bertha competed in the Cheyenne Frontier Days Celebration. She was the first woman to win a bronco-riding prize. After she won that prize, more women competed in rodeos. Bertha joined the Pawnee Bill Wild West Show in 1906. In the show, she rode broncos and did trick-riding. Being in that show made her a famous cowgirl.

Bertha also competed in Pendelton Round-Up competitions. She was an "all-around cowgirl" from 1911 to 1918. This is because she won so many events. She won relay races, trick-riding events, and the Cowgirl's Bucking Contest. In 1914, Bertha almost won the title of all-around cowboy! That means she did better than most of the men, too.

Bertha was married to Del Blanchett. They starred together in many silent films about the Wild West. Because of her work, Bertha Blanchett won a place in the National Cowboy Hall of Fame. She is also in the Pendelton Round-Up Hall of Fame and the National Cowgirl Hall of Fame. What a great rider!

1 **Why was this story written?**

Ⓐ to explain what a rodeo is

Ⓑ to tell about a famous cowgirl

Ⓒ to talk about Wild West movies

Ⓓ to get you to go to a rodeo

2 **If you want to learn more about cowgirls, you should—**

Ⓕ read a book about women of the West

Ⓖ read an article about broncos

Ⓗ find out where Pendelton is

Ⓙ look up "rodeo" in an encyclopedia

3 **This story could also be called—**

Ⓐ "Wild Wild Horses"

Ⓑ "The Pendelton Round-Up"

Ⓒ "Pawnee Bill and Friends"

Ⓓ "A Rodeo Cowgirl"

4 **Bertha joined the Pawnee Bill Wild West Show in —**

Ⓕ 1906

Ⓖ 1911

Ⓗ 1914

Ⓙ 1918

5 **What is explained in the last paragraph?**

Ⓐ Who is Bertha Blanchett?

Ⓑ Which Halls of Fame honor Bertha?

Ⓒ When did Bertha compete in the Pendelton Round-Up?

Ⓓ Where was Bertha born?

Flea Market & Sales   2600

FLEA MARKET

Fun for all ages!

The New City Lion's Club will hold a Flea Market on Saturday, June 21 and Sunday, June 22. The Flea Market will be in the New City Mall parking lot.

The rain dates are June 28 and 29.

The Flea Market opens at 10:00 A.M. and closes at 6:00 P.M.

Jewelry, Crafts, Clothes, Toys, Plants, and many more items will all be for sale. There will be special booths for baby clothes and toys.

Tickets for the flea market will be $2.00 for adults and children over 6 years old. Children 6 and under get in free. No one without a ticket may enter.

If you want to rent a booth, or help at the food booth, please call Mrs. Johnson at 555-1234.

There will be booths selling food, soda, and snacks. Hot coffee and tea will be free. There will be picnic tables and chairs.

6 **Who should you call if you want to rent a booth?**

- Ⓕ The New City Lion's Club
- Ⓖ The Flea Market
- Ⓗ Mrs. Johnson
- Ⓙ The New City Mall

7 **Which of the following items is not mentioned in the notice?**

- Ⓐ Crafts
- Ⓑ Toys
- Ⓒ Plants
- Ⓓ Books

8 **Where will the Flea Market take place?**

- Ⓕ The New City Lion's Club
- Ⓖ The New City Mall
- Ⓗ In a parking lot
- Ⓙ At the local school

9 **On which day will the Flea Market open to the public?**

- Ⓐ June 21
- Ⓑ June 28
- Ⓒ June 29
- Ⓓ June 30

Directions

Read each passage and answer the questions that follow.

Native American Rattle

Everyone likes playing music. Here's a musical instrument that you can make yourself. It's easy and fun.

Here's what you need:

Two paper cups

Dry beans

Masking tape

Markers

Glue

Newspaper

Two hours

First, decorate one of the paper cups. You can draw on the cup with markers or make a design in glitter. To do this, first draw a design in glue. Then, sprinkle glitter on top of the glue. Be sure to cover the glue completely with glitter. Shake the extra glitter onto a piece of newspaper. Decorate the second paper cup. Wait one hour for the glue to dry.

Fill both cups half way with the dry beans. Tape the two cups together.

Now you are ready to make some music.

1 The first step is to—
- Ⓐ use white glue
- Ⓑ fill the paper cups with dry beans
- Ⓒ decorate the paper cup with designs
- Ⓓ tape the paper cups together

2 The glitter is used to—
- Ⓕ remove the white glue
- Ⓖ fill one of the paper cups
- Ⓗ mix with the white glue
- Ⓙ cover the white glue

3 It is important to use dry beans for the rattle to—
- Ⓐ become heavy
- Ⓑ make noise
- Ⓒ stick together
- Ⓓ be pretty

4 How long would it take you to make a Native American rattle?
- Ⓕ Two hours
- Ⓖ 1 hour
- Ⓗ Half a day
- Ⓙ The story does not say.

5 If you are interested in finding similar activities, it is best to—
- Ⓐ go to the toy store
- Ⓑ look at a children's crafts book
- Ⓒ read a history book
- Ⓓ visit a museum

6 If you don't have a newspaper, you can probably use —
- Ⓕ markers
- Ⓖ some beans
- Ⓗ a fork
- Ⓙ a paper towel

Chewing Gum

It's soft. It's chewy. It tastes good, but you can't eat it. Can you guess what it is?

It's chewing gum.

At first, chewing gum came from a special tree called the sapodilla tree. Now people make gum base from synthetic (manmade) and natural ingredients. These ingredients are melted together to make a sticky substance.

Sweeteners, flavorings, and colorings are added to the gum base. Most chewing gum uses powdered sugar or syrups. Bubble gum may be colored with pink dye, while green dye may be added to mint gum. The candy maker may also add spices or fruit juice to the gum base to give the gum flavor.

After this warm mixture thickens, it is put into an <u>extruder</u>. This machine blends and smooths the gum.

Next, the gum needs to be shaped. It can be cut into sticks, chunks, or other shapes. Then it is sprinkled with a powdered sweetener. This keeps it from sticking to the wrapper.

The gum needs to be cooled for two days. Then large machines quickly wrap and pack it in airtight packaging. This keeps the gum fresh and soft. Finally, it is shipped to stores for people to buy and chew.

7 In this passage, the word <u>extruder</u> is—

Ⓐ a mixture

Ⓑ a sweetener

Ⓒ a machine

Ⓓ a tree

8 The gum is sprinkled with a powdered sweetener so it—

Ⓕ will be sweet

Ⓖ will cool faster

Ⓗ can be cut into shapes

Ⓙ doesn't stick to things

9 To find out more about the history of chewing gum, you can —

Ⓐ go to the grocery store

Ⓑ read a book about factories

Ⓒ buy a pack of chewing gum

Ⓓ go to the library

10 You would probably read a story like this in an article called—

Ⓕ "The History of Latex"

Ⓖ "From the Sapodilla Tree to Pink Bubbles"

Ⓗ "A Fun Candy Recipe"

Ⓙ "Sugarless Snacks and Treats"

11 After the warm mixture thickens, it is—

Ⓐ melted and filtered

Ⓑ washed and cooled

Ⓒ blended and smoothed

Ⓓ packed and shipped

STOP

Directions
Read each passage and answer the questions that follow.

Dairy Farming in Maryland

Janine lives on a dairy farm in the state of Maryland. A dairy farm is where cows are raised for their milk. Janine's parents have sixty cows. They must milk the cows twice a day. That's a lot of milking!

Janine's parents wake up early. Every morning at five o'clock, they walk to the cow barn. The milking parlor is a very clean area inside the barn. There they milk the cows with an automatic machine. Using a machine is much faster than milking the cows by hand, one at a time. With the machine, Janine's parents can milk all of their cows in about an hour.

The milk goes from the machine into a refrigerated tank in the barn. Every other day, the milk is pumped into a special truck that comes to the farm. The truck takes the milk to a dairy company. Some of it will be made into butter. Most of the milk will be put into cartons, which are sold at grocery stores.

Janine's parents milk the cows again in the early evening. Each cow gives about six gallons of milk per day. That's a lot of milk! Janine's father says that the cows give so much milk because they are Holsteins. These black and white colored cows are a favorite <u>breed</u> among dairy farmers. Holstein cows eat a lot, but they give much more milk than other kinds of cows.

Janine likes living on a farm. She also likes drinking milk.

1 In this story, the word <u>breed</u> means—

Ⓐ color

Ⓑ milking machine

Ⓒ type of milk

Ⓓ kind of cow

2 How often is milk pumped into a truck?

Ⓕ Twice a day

Ⓖ Once a day

Ⓗ Every other day

Ⓙ Twice a week

3 The first paragraph of the story answers which of these questions?

Ⓐ Does Janine milk the cows?

Ⓑ How often do they milk the cows?

Ⓒ How long does it take to milk the cows?

Ⓓ When do they milk the cows?

4 The milking parlor is kept very clean because—

Ⓕ that is where the cows are milked

Ⓖ they brush the cows there

Ⓗ Janine likes to drink milk there

Ⓙ it is inside their house

5 The writer tells this story mainly to—

Ⓐ list Janine's chores

Ⓑ show what happens at a dairy farm

Ⓒ explain why farmers grow corn

Ⓓ describe how butter is made

Scavenger Hunt

This is a fun game to play with 2 or more friends. One person is the "Judge." The others are the "Finders."

Each Finder needs:

A pen or pencil

A piece of paper

A small bag

How to play:

1. The Judge thinks of several items. The Judge should choose things that are small and easy to find nearby.

2. The Judge tells the Finders what the items are. The finders write them down.

3. The Judge tells the Finders to start. The Finders look for each of the items on the list.

4. Each time Finders find an item, they put it in their bag.

5. When a Finder finds all of the items, he or she takes them back to the Judge.

6. The Judge checks to make sure the Finder has all of the right items. If he or she does, then that person is the winner.

7. The game can continue until all of the Finders bring back their items.

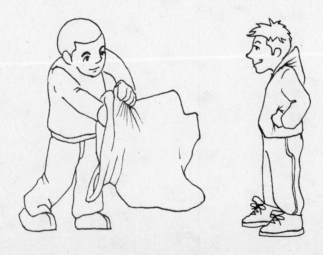

6 The game would be unfair if—

   Ⓕ there were more players

   Ⓖ each Finder had a different list of items

   Ⓗ if the Finders used backpacks instead of bags

   Ⓙ if one of the Finders had a pen and a pencil

7 How many Judges does this game need?

   Ⓐ One

   Ⓑ Two

   Ⓒ Three

   Ⓓ Seven

8 When you find an item, you—

   Ⓕ write down what the item is

   Ⓖ score a point

   Ⓗ put it in your bag

   Ⓙ bring it to the Judge

9 You take the items back to the Judge in step—

   Ⓐ 2

   Ⓑ 3

   Ⓒ 5

   Ⓓ 6

10 Which is not a good item for a judge to choose—

   Ⓕ a leaf

   Ⓖ a bottlecap

   Ⓗ a piece of string

   Ⓙ a piano

11 Games like this would probably be in a book titled —

   Ⓐ *Fun Outdoor Games*

   Ⓑ *Riddles for Kids*

   Ⓒ *Games You Can Play By Yourself*

   Ⓓ *Learn How to Draw*

STOP

Directions
Read each passage and answer the questions that follow.

An Incredible Sea Creature

Because its arms radiate outward from the center of its body, the starfish looks like a star. There are over a thousand different kinds of starfish. Most have five arms. Some have four. Some have six arms or more. Starfish range in size from about 1 centimeter wide to about 25 centimeters wide.

The starfish is an invertebrate. That means it does not have a backbone. Water-filled tubes run down the length of each arm. These tubes branch out into smaller tubes. The tubes support the body the way a skeleton supports other animals. The ends of the tubes form rows of "feet" on the bottom of the starfish. The tube feet allow the starfish to crawl.

The mouth of the starfish is on the same side as its feet, right in the center. The starfish eats many things. It can actually push its stomach out of its mouth to help it eat. To eat an oyster, the starfish pries open the two shells with its arms. Then it slips its stomach in between the shells.

---

1 The word invertebrate means that an animal —

Ⓐ lives underwater

Ⓑ cannot move

Ⓒ does not have a backbone

Ⓓ eats shellfish

2 To find out more about starfish, you should—

Ⓕ take a boat trip

Ⓖ read a dictionary

Ⓗ visit a dinosaur exhibit

Ⓙ look in the encyclopedia

3 Which question does the last paragraph of the story answer?

Ⓐ Where does the starfish live?

Ⓑ How big is the starfish?

Ⓒ How does the starfish eat?

Ⓓ How does the starfish move?

4 Most starfish have—

Ⓕ four arms

Ⓖ five arms

Ⓗ six arms

Ⓙ more than six arms

5 This story would probably be included in a book called—

Ⓐ *Mammals Great and Small*

Ⓑ *Wonders of Earth's Oceans*

Ⓒ *Amazing Feats of Magic*

Ⓓ *Underwater Plants*

6 What supports the starfish like a skeleton?

Ⓕ Water-filled tubes

Ⓖ Arms

Ⓗ Its mouth and stomach

Ⓙ Its backbone

The Keeper of History

Oladapo and his family live in New York. He is the youngest of five children. Oladapo's father comes from a small country in Africa. In his native country, Oladapo's father was the storyteller of the local village. He told old stories about the village that he learned from his father.

Every Sunday Oladapo's father would go to the village center to tell a story. The entire village would sit around and listen. Some of the stories were funny. Other stories were scary. But most of them were about events that happened in the village long ago. The storyteller was a very important man in the village. At the time, not too many books were available. The people in the village wanted to know the history of their village and the people who lived there before them. Oladapo's father was so important that he was like the second chief in the village.

In time, more schools were built and more books became available. Oladapo's father's position in the village changed. He was no longer the person who kept the history of the village alive. He became more of an entertainer. Still, people loved to hear his stories. When he came to the United States, he gave his job to his brother. In New York, though, Oladapo's father continues to tell stories to his family and friends.

7 The last paragraph answers which question?

Ⓐ Why did Oladapo's father position change in time?

Ⓑ How many people would listen to the stories?

Ⓒ Where does Oladapo's father come from?

Ⓓ What type of stories were mostly told?

8 Most of Oladapo's father's stories were about events that—

Ⓕ were funny

Ⓖ happened long ago

Ⓗ will happen in the future

Ⓘ people had forgotten

9 What is the purpose of this story?

Ⓐ To describe Oladapo's family

Ⓑ To tell us about the importance of storytellers

Ⓒ To get you to visit a library

Ⓓ To make you tell your own stories

10 Oladapo's father is regarded as a keeper of history because he—

Ⓕ told stories

Ⓖ is old

Ⓗ is important

Ⓘ knows all the events

11 If you wanted to find out more about storytellers, you should—

Ⓐ visit a museum

Ⓑ draw a picture of New York

Ⓒ read a book about African villages

Ⓓ study old stories

Directions

Read each passage and answer the questions that follow.

A Week with Heidi

One day Mrs. Posada, a neighbor, stopped Kirsten on her way home from school. She said that her family was going to go on a trip. Could Kirsten take care of their cat for a week?

Kirsten had fed Heidi before. She liked the cat. It sounded easy. Mrs. Posada wanted Kirsten to talk it over with her mother before deciding.

After talking with her mom, Kirsten realized what a big responsibility the job would be. A week is a long time. She would have to go over to the Posada's house every day. She would have to play with Heidi a little since the cat might get lonely. She would have to feed the cat and make sure it was okay.

Her mom said she could let Kirsten into the Posada's house each day. She would help out if the cat needed special attention. But Kirsten would have to do the basic tasks, feeding the cat and playing with it, herself. Kirsten agreed, and told Mrs. Posada the next day.

That weekend, Kirsten waved goodbye as her neighbors left on their long trip. For the next seven days, Kirsten fed Heidi. She pet Heidi. She played with Heidi. Usually she wanted to do it. A couple of times, she didn't really feel like it, but each day she took care of the cat no matter how she felt.

When the family returned, Mrs. Posada came over. She said that Heidi looked great. Mrs. Posada said she was proud of Kirsten for doing such a good job. "Thank you," said Mrs. Posada. She handed Kirsten a large box wrapped in bright yellow paper. "This is for you. Go ahead, open it," Mrs. Posada said.

1 The day after speaking with her mom about the job, Kirsten—

Ⓐ told Mrs. Posada that she would take care of the cat

Ⓑ still could not decide what to do

Ⓒ waved goodbye to the Posada family

Ⓓ began to feed Heidi each day

2 Why did Mrs. Posada give Kirsten a gift?

Ⓕ It was Kirsten's birthday.

Ⓖ Kirsten earned good grades in school.

Ⓗ She wanted to thank Kirsten for taking care of Heidi.

Ⓙ She wanted Kirsten to keep the cat.

3 You can tell that Mrs. Posada felt like—

Ⓐ her family's cat was getting older

Ⓑ Kirsten could be trusted

Ⓒ they really shouldn't have gone on the trip

Ⓓ Kirsten's family might move out of the neighborhood

4 After talking with her mom, Kirsten realized that the job—

Ⓕ would be more involved than she first thought

Ⓖ was too easy for her

Ⓗ was too difficult for her

Ⓙ would interfere with school

5 What will Kirsten probably do next in the story?

Ⓐ Go find Heidi

Ⓑ Hand the box to her mother

Ⓒ Give the box back to Mrs. Posada

Ⓓ Open the box

6 What other title would be good for this story?

Ⓕ "Kirsten Gets a Yellow Box"

Ⓖ "Nursing Heidi Back to Health"

Ⓗ "Caring for a Cat is a Big Job"

Ⓙ "The Posada Family's Great Adventure"

Jon and the Tree House

Jon was great at building things. He thought he was the best builder in the neighborhood. Once he built a skateboard ramp all by himself. But he never let his friends help him.

Jon decided he wanted a tree house. He thought the best place for it was in the big tree in his backyard. His friends talked about what kind of tree house they would build, but Jon said he would do it himself. Jon told his friends that after he built it, he would invite them over.

When he tried to build the tree house, Jon had many problems. He tried to hoist the boards up with a rope. It kept getting tangled in the branches. He tried to nail a board to the trunk. He kept dropping it. Jon never had so much trouble before. He wondered what he should do.

Jon's friends came over to see how he was doing. They saw him drop his hammer. Patti picked it up and handed it back. Jon looked embarrassed when he took it. Later he tried to push a large board up the tree, but he could not do it. Andy went over and helped him. After a few minutes, they got the board up the tree.

After awhile, they figured out a good system. Patti handed up the supplies. Andy held the boards in place. Jon nailed them together. Because they cooperated, the tree house was built more quickly. By the end of the day, it was almost finished. Jon was glad that he let his friends help. They got more done, and they had fun!

---

7 Jon's friends came over because they wanted to know—

Ⓐ which tree he was using

Ⓑ if he was embarrassed

Ⓒ when he would be finished

Ⓓ how he was doing

8 What would be another possible title for the story?

Ⓕ "A Long Summer"

Ⓖ "Jon's Skateboard Ramp"

Ⓗ "Cooperation Counts"

Ⓙ "New Friends"

9 Why did Jon tell his friends that he would invite them over after he finished?

Ⓐ He wanted some help later.

Ⓑ They had other things to do that afternoon.

Ⓒ He didn't want them to help him build the tree house.

Ⓓ He wanted to go skateboarding with them.

10 You can tell from the story that Jon learned—

Ⓕ how to make friends

Ⓖ what supplies he needed to build a tree house

Ⓗ how to climb a tree

Ⓙ that it's important to cooperate sometimes

11 Jon didn't ask for any help because—

Ⓐ he thought he was the best builder in the neighborhood

Ⓑ Patti wasn't a good builder

Ⓒ Andy was too busy to help

Ⓓ it was going to be his tree house

STOP

Directions

Read each passage and answer the questions that follow.

The Lion and the Mouse

In ancient Greece, there was a man named Aesop. He is famous for telling many fables. Here is one of his more popular fables.

Once while a great Lion was sleeping, a little Mouse ran up and down his back. The Lion woke with a great roar. "Who is playing on my back?" he asked and he stretched out his great paw. The Lion caught the little Mouse beneath his paw.

"How dare you bother me while I'm sleeping!" said the Lion. "For that I will eat you!" The Lion opened his mouth to swallow the Mouse.

"I'm sorry," the little Mouse squealed. "Forgive me and I won't ever forget it. Who knows, maybe I will be able to do a favor for you someday."

The Lion laughed and said "Oh, you silly little Mouse! How could you ever help me?" Laughing put the lion in a good mood and he let the Mouse go free.

A few weeks later, the Lion was caught in a hunter's trap. The hunter wanted to take him to the King. They tied the lion to a tree while they looked for a wagon to carry him on.

"Oh no, I am doomed," the Lion said to himself. The Mouse happened to be close enough to hear him.

So the Mouse came over and asked the great Lion "What is the matter?"

"I've been captured by hunters," the Lion answered. "They are coming back for me soon."

"Well, it is time for me to return the favor," the Mouse said. He started to chew away at the rope that was tied to the Lion's foot. He chewed and he chewed until the rope broke in two.

The Lion was so thrilled. "You were able to help me little Mouse. Thank you!"

"You are welcome," the Mouse replied.

"If you ever need a favor, please let me know," the Lion said. The Lion and the Mouse became good friends and they helped each other whenever they could.

1 What is the lesson of this story?

Ⓐ Never talk to strangers.

Ⓑ Look before you leap.

Ⓒ Little friends may prove to be great friends.

Ⓓ Beware of unseen traps.

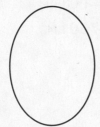

The Lion is caught in a trap.   The Mouse frees the Lion.

2 Which of these should go in Circle 2?

Ⓕ The Mouse hears the Lion.

Ⓖ The Lion frees the Mouse.

Ⓗ The Mouse runs up and down the Lion's back.

Ⓙ The Lion and the Mouse become friends.

3 Aesop probably told fables like this to—

Ⓐ make people laugh

Ⓑ show how animals act

Ⓒ teach lessons about life

Ⓓ make people like animals more

4 How was the Lion set free?

Ⓕ The Lion climbed up the tree.

Ⓖ The hunters never came back.

Ⓗ The Mouse untied the rope.

Ⓙ The Mouse chewed through the rope.

5 The Lion originally thought that—

Ⓐ the hunters couldn't catch him

Ⓑ the Mouse was too small to be helpful

Ⓒ the Mouse was smart

Ⓓ the King would show mercy

6 By reading this story, you can tell that a fable is—

Ⓕ a poem about animals

Ⓖ a story that happened a long time ago

Ⓗ a true story about animals

Ⓙ a make-believe story about animals

7 By the end of the story, the Mouse probably felt —

Ⓐ sorry

Ⓑ helpful

Ⓒ scared

Ⓓ funny

Summer Day Camp Schedule

MEALS

Breakfast*	7:00–8:00 A.M.
Lunch	12:00–1:00 P.M.
Dinner	6:30–7:30 P.M.

* Brunch is served on Sunday, 10:00–11:00 A.M. instead of
   Breakfast and Lunch

SPORTS

Tuesday: *
Tennis with Ms. Jones   3:30–5:30 P.M.
at the tennis courts

Thursday *
Swimming with Ms. Morgen   3:00–6:00 P.M.
at Little Pond,

Saturday
Basketball with Mr. Burger   3:30–5:30 P.M.
at the gym

* If it rains on Tuesday or Thursday, then meet at the gym to play basketball.

RECREATION

Wednesday:
Horseshoes with Mr. Sims   3:00–5:00 P.M.
at North Field

Friday:
Hiking with Mr. Sims   3:00–6:00 P.M.
meet at North Field

Sunday:
Canoeing with Ms. Morgen   3:00–6:00 P.M.
at Little Pond

8 Who is in charge of canoeing?

   Ⓕ Mr. Sims

   Ⓖ Mr. Burger

   Ⓗ Ms. Morgen

   Ⓙ Ms. Jones

9 Which day is hiking planned?

   Ⓐ Monday

   Ⓑ Wednesday

   Ⓒ Friday

   Ⓓ Saturday

10 If it rains, campers will play —

   Ⓕ tennis

   Ⓖ basketball

   Ⓗ swimming

   Ⓙ horseshoes

11 Where could you find this schedule?

   Ⓐ In a comic book

   Ⓑ On television

   Ⓒ In a newspaper

   Ⓓ In the camp's cafeteria

12 Where does the hiking begin?

   Ⓕ at the gym

   Ⓖ at North Field

   Ⓗ by Little Pond

   Ⓙ by the tennis courts

STOP

PRACTICE TEST

DIRECTIONS

Read the passages. Then, use the information to answer the questions below.

SAMPLES A & B

Dog's Mistake

Darby Dog was going to the forest to see Francie Fox. He heard that Francie Fox wasn't feeling well lately. He was going to bring him some flowers. "These flowers will cheer Francie Fox up," Darby Dog said.

When Darby Dog got to Francie Fox's house, Francie Fox was outside jumping rope. "The flowers are very pretty," Fox said, "But I feel fine! SuSu Squirrel is the one who doesn't feel well."

"Oh my," said Darby Dog, "I feel so silly!"

"You shouldn't feel silly," Francie Fox said, "Everyone makes mistakes."

"Well, as long as I have these flowers," Darby Dog said, "we should go give them to Squirrel."

"That sounds like a great idea!" said Francie Fox. So they both went to visit SuSu Squirrel.

A **Who was Darby Dog going to visit first?**

Ⓐ SuSu Squirrel

Ⓑ Francie Fox

Ⓒ Barry Bear

Ⓓ Chuck Chipmunk

B **How did Darby Dog feel when he found out Francie Fox wasn't sick?**

Ⓕ angry

Ⓖ sad

Ⓗ happy

Ⓙ foolish

Railroad Schedule

Trains Arriving From			Trains Departing To		

Trains Arriving From

TIME	TRACK	CITY
10 A.M.	Track 2	Los Angeles
11 A.M.	Track 4	Chicago
1 P.M.	Track 1	Houston
3 P.M.	Track 5	Denver
4 P.M.	Track 3	New York
5 P.M.	Track 2	Boston
9 P.M.	Track 4	Cleveland

No trains will arrive after 9 P.M. due to work to be performed on tracks.

Trains Departing To

TIME	TRACK	CITY
9 A.M	Track 6	Atlanta
10 A.M	Track 8	Boston
12 Noon	Track 9	Denver
2 P.M.	Track 10	Cleveland
4 P.M.	Track 7	Houston
5 P.M.	Track 6	New York
8 P.M.	Track 8	Chicago

No trains will depart after 8 P.M. due to work to be performed on tracks.

No tickets sold after 7 P.M.

For more information on arriving trains, call 555-3333.

For more information on departing trains, call 555-4444.

---

1 What city will you go to if you are on the train that leaves at 10 A.M.?

Ⓐ Los Angeles

Ⓑ Atlanta

Ⓒ Boston

Ⓓ Cleveland

2 What city can you go to, but not come from?

Ⓕ Los Angeles

Ⓖ Chicago

Ⓗ Atlanta

Ⓙ Cleveland

3 What is the latest time that you can buy your ticket?

Ⓐ 9 A.M.

Ⓑ 7 P.M.

Ⓒ 4 P.M.

Ⓓ 10 A.M.

4 When will the railroad station be the least busy?

Ⓕ 5 P.M.

Ⓖ 10 A.M.

Ⓗ 6 A.M.

Ⓙ 1 P.M.

5 To find out about the train going to Atlanta, which would you do?

Ⓐ Call the library

Ⓑ Call 555-4444

Ⓒ Call 555-3333

Ⓓ Call the post office

The Liberty Bell

The Liberty Bell is one of the most famous objects from the Revolutionary War. This was the war in which the United States won its independence from the British. The Liberty Bell was used to tell people when something important happened. Remember, it was a time when there was no television or radio. There were newspapers, but they didn't come out every day. At the time, the Liberty Bell was the fastest and easiest way to tell people news. Over the years, it became a symbol for freedom.

The Liberty Bell was made in Pennsylvania.. It was first rung in 1753. The bell did not work well when it was first made. In fact, the bell cracked the first time it was used! Copper was added to the bottom of the bell to make it stronger. The bell was used to summon people together for special announcements and events.

Later, the bell was rung for the Boston Tea Party and for the Declaration of Independence. During the war, the British took over Philadelphia. The bell had to be hidden so it would not be captured. The bell was hidden in Allentown, Pennsylvania, underneath the floor of a church. The bell was brought back to Philadelphia when the war was over.

The bell was again used to tell people important news. In 1846, the bell cracked badly when it was rung for George Washington's birthday. It could not be rung again. What would be done with this important part of United States history? A decision was made to put the bell in a museum where everybody could see it. Ever since then, the bell has been on display for the public.

6 Why was the Liberty Bell hidden during the Revolutionary War?

    Ⓕ Because there was no television

    Ⓖ Because it has a crack in it

    Ⓗ So it could not be stolen

    Ⓙ So it could not tell people news

7 Why was the Liberty Bell put in a museum?

    Ⓐ To tell people news that had just happened

    Ⓑ Because radio and television were invented

    Ⓒ There was no more news for the bell to announce

    Ⓓ Because the bell was an important piece of American history

8 What did the copper do to the Liberty Bell?

    Ⓕ Helped the bell last longer

    Ⓖ Made the bell crack

    Ⓗ Made it harder for the British to find

    Ⓙ Made the bell bigger

9 To answer question 8, which should the reader do?

    Ⓐ Read the title of the story again.

    Ⓑ Go to a museum to see if the Liberty Bell is there.

    Ⓒ Scan the story for the word "copper."

    Ⓓ Reread the first paragraph of the story.

10 For which of the following was the Liberty Bell rung?

    Ⓕ When it was put in a museum

    Ⓖ The Boston Tea Party

    Ⓗ When it cracked

    Ⓙ To tell the British where it was hiding

The Big Hill

Derek saw the big hill beyond the end of his street everyday. No one could miss it. It was so high! You could probably see everything from up there!

Derek wanted to go up the hill. His older brother and sister had climbed it. But Derek's parents thought he was too young to go up the hill by himself. "You will be old enough soon," Derek's father said. Derek wondered when *soon* would arrive. Derek could climb the pine tree at the end of the street. Derek could see the whole street from the tree. But the big hill was so much higher!

Derek did well on his last report card of the year. His parents were pleased. They had a surprise for him. They told Derek they would climb up the big hill with him because he had done so well in school. "All the way to the top?" Derek asked. "Right to the top," Derek's mother said.

When they left, Derek and his parents walked to the end of the street. This time, they walked past the pine tree. The path started a few steps beyond the pine tree. After a few minutes of walking, the path became steep. Derek was glad he brought the water. He had to stop and drink from it several times. Even his parents were sweating. It was a really hard climb!

An hour passed. The path led to an area where there were no trees. Derek had reached the top. He looked down at his street. There was his house. It looked so small from up there! There was the supermarket. There was the school. This was better than the pine tree. You really could see everything from up there! He wondered what his friends would say when he told them he had climbed the hill.

11 **What was at the end of the street?**

    Ⓐ   The school

    Ⓑ   The supermarket

    Ⓒ   Derek's house

    Ⓓ   The pine tree

12 **Why was Derek sweating?**

    Ⓕ   Because he didn't climb the pine tree

    Ⓖ   Because climbing was hard work

    Ⓗ   Because he had water in his backpack

    Ⓙ   Because he was by himself

13 **Why did Derek want to climb the hill?**

    Ⓐ   You could see better from the top of the hill.

    Ⓑ   The trees were not as big at the top of the hill.

    Ⓒ   You needed a backpack to go to the top of the hill.

    Ⓓ   Derek thought he could beat his friend to the top.

14 **Why did Derek walk up the path?**

    Ⓕ   The path was a shortcut to the supermarket.

    Ⓖ   The path went past the pine tree.

    Ⓗ   Walking the path would keep him in the shade.

    Ⓙ   The path led to the top of the big hill.

15 **Which of the following will probably happen next?**

    Ⓐ   Derek will tell his friends what he saw from the top of the hill.

    Ⓑ   Derek will decide not to wear his backpack again.

    Ⓒ   Derek will go home and climb the pine tree a lot more.

    Ⓓ   Derek's parents will move to the top of the hill.

DIRECTIONS

Look at the underlined word in each question. Then, choose the answer that is closest in meaning to the underlined word.

SAMPLE A

A A <u>silent</u> person is a person who is—

- Ⓐ thoughtful
- Ⓑ quiet
- Ⓒ angry
- Ⓓ serious

1 A <u>sofa</u> is a kind of—

- Ⓐ lamp
- Ⓑ room
- Ⓒ couch
- Ⓓ pillow

2 To <u>glance</u> at something is to—

- Ⓕ fight against it
- Ⓖ look at it
- Ⓗ wait for it
- Ⓙ play with it

3 To <u>eliminate</u> something is to—

- Ⓐ understand it
- Ⓑ remove it
- Ⓒ control it
- Ⓓ begin it

4 A <u>saucer</u> is a type of—

- Ⓕ tool
- Ⓖ plate
- Ⓗ house
- Ⓙ cup

5 To <u>construct</u> something is to—

- Ⓐ build it
- Ⓑ destroy it
- Ⓒ imagine it
- Ⓓ carry it

6 Something that is <u>enormous</u> is—

- Ⓕ difficult
- Ⓖ large
- Ⓗ tiny
- Ⓙ lovely

7 A <u>location</u> is a—

- Ⓐ place
- Ⓑ person
- Ⓒ job
- Ⓓ treasure

8 To <u>pretend</u> is to—

- Ⓕ make a copy of
- Ⓖ play with
- Ⓗ make believe
- Ⓙ look after

9 To <u>trap</u> something is to—

- Ⓐ frighten it
- Ⓑ know about it
- Ⓒ spy on it
- Ⓓ catch it

10 To <u>enjoy</u> something means to—

- Ⓕ like it
- Ⓖ feed it
- Ⓗ sell it
- Ⓙ end it

11 A <u>solution</u> is a kind of—

Ⓐ problem

Ⓑ answer

Ⓒ question

Ⓓ complaint

12 To <u>leap</u> is to—

Ⓕ run

Ⓖ sleep

Ⓗ play

Ⓘ jump

13 A <u>grin</u> is most like a—

Ⓐ bush

Ⓑ smile

Ⓒ cat

Ⓓ tool

14 To <u>carve</u> means to—

Ⓕ wait

Ⓖ fix

Ⓗ cut

Ⓘ fill

15 A <u>ranch</u> is most like a—

Ⓐ museum

Ⓑ captain

Ⓒ bench

Ⓓ farm

16 A <u>tale</u> is —

Ⓕ a story

Ⓖ an animal

Ⓗ a friend

Ⓘ a market

17 To <u>broil</u> means to—

Ⓐ hide

Ⓑ break

Ⓒ cook

Ⓓ use

18 A <u>braid</u> is like a—

Ⓕ knot

Ⓖ knife

Ⓗ foot

Ⓘ lake

DIRECTIONS

Read the sentence in the box. Then, choose the answer where the underlined word is used in the same way as it is in the box.

SAMPLE B

B

> **My cousin can only swim one lap in the pool.**

Which answer uses the word lap in the same way as it is above?

Ⓐ I put the napkin in my lap as I slid my chair under the table.

Ⓑ I watched the kitten lap up the dish of milk.

Ⓒ Carmen has one more lap around the track to go.

Ⓓ Listen to the ocean waves lap against the side of the boat.

19

> **How fast do you think that car can go?**

Which answer uses the word fast in the same way as it is above?

Ⓐ It is hard to fast because you cannot eat or drink a thing.

Ⓑ My offer is hard and fast, so take it or leave it.

Ⓒ Geoffrey is a very fast runner.

Ⓓ The prisoner's cell was locked up fast.

20

> **The bill at the restaurant was more expensive than I thought.**

Which answer uses the word bill in the same way as it is above?

Ⓕ The plumber sent us a bill for his work.

Ⓖ That bird had a very large bill.

Ⓗ The bill was passed in Congress and became a law.

Ⓙ There were four musicians on the bill that evening.

21

> **This plain white T-shirt doesn't have any designs on it.**

Which answer uses the word plain in the same way as it is above?

Ⓐ The farmer planted his summer crops on the plain.

Ⓑ The teacher asked us to take out some plain paper.

Ⓒ Be plain with me and tell me the truth right now.

Ⓓ The answer is as plain as the nose on your face.

22

> **Try not to make such a mess when you eat!**

Which answer uses the word mess in the same way as it is above?

Ⓕ You shouldn't mess around with something that isn't yours.

Ⓖ "Don't mess with me!" the cowboy said to the villain.

Ⓗ Mom told my brother and me that we had to clean up the mess we made.

Ⓙ While in the army, the soldiers ate their meals in the mess hall.

23

> **Every shelf in my bookcase is filled.**

Which answer uses the word shelf in the same way as it is above?

Ⓐ Could you put this box back on the shelf for me?

Ⓑ "We're going to put that topic on the shelf," the lawyer said.

Ⓒ There is a shelf of limestone in that mine.

Ⓓ Canned food has a long shelf life.

DIRECTIONS

Read the sentences below. Use the sentence to figure out the meaning of the underlined word. Then, choose the answer that best shows what the underlined word means.

SAMPLE C

C After trying to keep up with you all day, I am <u>exhausted</u>. <u>Exhausted</u> means—

Ⓐ dirty
Ⓑ active
Ⓒ tired
Ⓓ strong

24 The <u>courageous</u> captain saved the ship from the terrible storm. <u>Courageous</u> means—

Ⓕ ridiculous
Ⓖ timid
Ⓗ brave
Ⓙ clumsy

25 The problem is so <u>complicated</u> that I do not think I will ever figure it out. <u>Complicated</u> means—

Ⓐ easy
Ⓑ intelligent
Ⓒ difficult
Ⓓ large

26 Rico's <u>hilarious</u> joke made us all laugh until our sides hurt. <u>Hilarious</u> means—

Ⓕ harmful
Ⓖ disgusting
Ⓗ funny
Ⓙ insulting

27 The <u>monstrous</u> boat has enough room for ten thousand passengers. <u>Monstrous</u> means—

Ⓐ hidden
Ⓑ gigantic
Ⓒ silly
Ⓓ small

28 I made my sister so <u>furious</u> that she would not talk to me for three days. <u>Furious</u> means—

Ⓕ angry
Ⓖ happy
Ⓗ pretty
Ⓙ tired

STOP

FIVE DAYS TO THE STANFORD-9

Welcome to the final stage of preparation for the Reading Vocabulary and Reading Comprehension sections of the Stanford-9 test. You began by taking a Practice Test that will help you prepare for the actual test that you will take. The Practice Test will help you learn to pace yourself and will provide you with a sneak preview of what the actual test-taking experience will be like.

After correcting your test, you will learn some test-taking tips and strategies (also known as techniques) designed to help you do your best on the test. Over the next couple of weeks, you will learn more about the test and will have the chance to ask any questions that you have about the test.

In addition to teaching you new ways to find the best answer to questions on the actual test, there will be a practice exercise with several practice questions at the end of each technique section. Use these questions to practice the technique you have just learned.

What will be on the Reading Vocabulary and Reading Comprehension sections of the Stanford-9?

The Reading Vocabulary and Reading Comprehension sections of the Stanford-9 test have multiple-choice questions that test your vocabulary and ability to understand different types of written passages.

Number of Questions

Each question on the test has four answer choices for you to choose from. You will need to be able to identify and pick the best answer from among these four choices. The best answer is always provided for you on the Stanford-9. You will not have to come up with it yourself. You will only have to recognize it.

The number of questions on your test will depend on which version of the Stanford-9 your class takes. No matter how many questions there are, however, all of them will be multiple choice.

What's special about a multiple-choice test?

On a multiple-choice test like the Stanford-9, each question is followed by several answer choices. Your job is to find the best answer from among those choices.

Finding the correct answer on a multiple-choice test is easier than on a test where you have to fill in the answer yourself. The correct choice is always right in front of you. You just have to find it from among the choices given.

This book will help make multiple-choice tests easier for you. You will learn some important techniques to use when taking this type of test and you will get a chance to practice using these techniques. You will also get used to the special types of questions you will see on the Stanford-9 test.

Through practice and review, you will be able to do your best on the Stanford-9 test!

Good luck, and have fun!

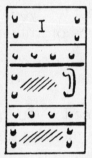 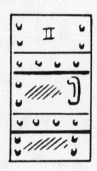 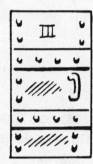 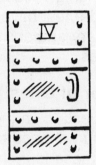

General Techniques

The Stanford-9 is a timed test, though the amount of time you will have to take the test will depend on how many questions are on the version of the test that your class will take. Your teacher will tell you how many questions will be on your test and how much time you will have. If your teacher does not tell you how many questions there will be on the test, don't be shy—ask! You will be more comfortable and will be able to concentrate on the test itself if you have this information.

Pace Yourself

Because the Stanford-9 is a timed test, you want to be sure to move through the questions at a good pace, or speed, in order to answer as many questions as possible. This doesn't mean that you need to race. It does mean that you need to make sure you keep working at a good rate. Remember that the more carefully you read the passages and questions the first time through, the less time you will have to spend in trying to understand what you have read.

Pacing yourself means keeping track in your mind of how much time you are spending to answer each question. You will want to make sure that you do not spend too long on questions that are difficult for you. Time that you spend on those questions could be better spent answering questions that are easier for you. By keeping track of time, you can be sure to finish as much of the test as possible.

Answer as many questions as you can. Sometimes it is helpful to answer the easier questions first. However, when you are finished with the easier questions, you must go back and guess at the answers to as many difficult questions as time permits. It is always better to take your best guess than not to answer the question at all.

Spend your time wisely. Don't use too much time answering any one question. If you don't know the correct answer to a question, take your best guess and then move on.

Ruling Out Wrong Answers

On a test such as the Stanford-9, your job is to find the best answer to each question. When you are not sure which choice is best, getting rid of bad choices can help you focus only on those answer choices that can answer the question correctly.

Here's a question for you to try to answer:

 1 **What is Jack's favorite season?**

Since we don't know Jack, the answer to this question could be anything.

Once we have answer choices, we can start ruling out those choices that cannot possibly make sense. Here is how:

Let's take a look at the answer choices.

    Ⓐ   history

    Ⓑ   library

    Ⓒ   red

    Ⓓ   winter

Look at choice *A*. Is *history* a season? No, it's not. It's a subject you learn in school. You can rule out answer choice *A*.

Look at choice *B*. Is *library* a season? No, it's not. It's a place. You can rule out answer choice *B*.

Look at choice *C*. Is *red* a season? No, it's not. It's a color. You can rule out answer choice *C*.

Look at choice *D*. Is *winter* a season? Yes, it is. Answer choice *D* is the correct answer.

By looking at the choices, and getting rid of wrong ones, you'll be able to find the best answer. You didn't even have to search for it! Practice this technique and use it whenever you are having even a little bit of difficulty answering a question.

 Working carefully prevents careless errors. If you work in this way, you should still be able to finish the test on time.

Now let's see how ruling out wrong answers could have helped you on the practice test. Remember, everything that you learn here will be useful to you when you take the real Stanford-9 test.

Let's answer the sample question from the practice test with this method.

---

1 **After trying to keep up with you all day, I am <u>exhausted</u>. <u>Exhausted</u> means—**

Ⓐ correct

Ⓑ active

Ⓒ tired

Ⓓ strong

If you're not sure what *exhausted* means, you can look at the answer choices.

Look at choice *A*. Could *correct* mean *exhausted*? Could you be *correct* from trying to keep up with someone? No, that doesn't make sense. You can rule out answer choice *A*.

Look at choice *B*. Could *active* mean *exhausted*? Could you be *active* from trying to keep up with someone? No, that doesn't make sense. You can rule out answer choice *B*.

Look at choice *C*. Could *tired* mean *exhausted*? Could you be *tired* from trying to keep up with someone? Yes, that could make sense. But, let's take a look at the last answer choice before we decide.

Look at choice *D*. Could *strong* mean *exhausted*? Could you be *strong* from trying to keep up with someone? No, that doesn't make sense. You can rule out answer choice *D*. Answer choice *C* is the correct answer.

Ruling out wrong answers leaves you with the best answer.

Remember, sometimes ruling out wrong answers will help you get rid of all but one answer choice. Other times, it will help you get rid of one or two answers. In those cases, you can make a good guess from the choices that are left.

 Remember to read all the answer choices carefully, even if you think you have already found the correct one. By looking at the choices and getting rid of wrong ones, you'll be able to find the best answer.

Try some more practice on these questions.

1 Cindy was so <u>bashful</u> that she didn't talk to anyone.
<u>Bashful</u> means—

Ⓐ friendly

Ⓑ silly

Ⓒ shy

Ⓓ old

2 I wanted my mom to tell me the secret, but she stayed <u>mute</u>.
<u>Mute</u> means—

Ⓕ walking

Ⓖ grinning

Ⓗ cheerful

Ⓙ silent

3 The <u>minuscule</u> chair wasn't even big enough for a baby.
<u>Minuscule</u> means—

Ⓐ capable

Ⓑ weird

Ⓒ broken

Ⓓ tiny

4 The operation was <u>transferred</u> from one part of town to another.
<u>Transferred</u> means—

Ⓕ moved

Ⓖ located

Ⓗ charged

Ⓙ filled

READING VOCABULARY

How to Prepare for Reading Vocabulary

✔ **The more words you know, the better**. Try to learn several new words every day. Read magazines, books, and newspapers. Look up the definitions of all the words you don't know.

✔ **Keep index cards of new words**. Write the definition of the word on the back of the card. Carry the cards with you and test yourself with them.

✔ **Use your new words in a sentence**. It is much harder to remember information if you don't have anything to use it for. Make it easy for yourself by trying to use these words in your everyday speech. That's what words are for!

There are three parts of the Reading Vocabulary section. They are:

- The **Synonym** section: You will need to pick a word that means the same thing as the word that is underlined.

- The **Multiple Definitions** section: You will need to know the different ways that the same word can be used. You will be given enough information to be able to identify how a given word is used. Then you will need to find the answer choice that uses that word in the same way.

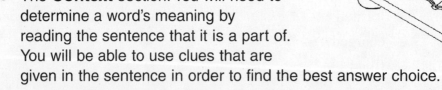

- The **Context** section: You will need to determine a word's meaning by reading the sentence that it is a part of. You will be able to use clues that are given in the sentence in order to find the best answer choice.

Now we will give you some more information about each of the three sections of the *Reading Vocabulary* section of the Stanford-9.

Synonyms

Synonyms are different words that mean that same thing. Some examples of synonyms are *friend* and *pal.* They are two different words which you can use to say almost the same thing.

The questions on this part of the Stanford-9 show you a phrase with an underlined word followed by four answer choices. You need to decide which one of the four answer choices has the same meaning, or a meaning that is close to the same meaning, as that of the underlined word.

Take a look at this question and its answer choices:

 1 To <u>conceal</u> something is to—

Ⓐ keep it

Ⓑ confuse it

Ⓒ buy it

Ⓓ hide it

To answer this question you should:

1. **Cover the answer choices and read the phrase**. This will help you to think about the question without worrying about looking for the answer.

    Some of the choices are included to confuse or distract you. In the above example, although *conceal* and *confuse* both begin with the same letters, they do not mean the same thing. The people who make the test put in words they think will trick you or make it difficult for you to find the best answer. After all, they are trying to test you! Be smart and take the time to think about what the best choice could be.

2. **Try to come up with your own definition of the underlined word before you look at the answer choices**. For the above example, you might think: *To conceal means to cover.* If you don't know what the underlined word means, move on to the next step.

3. **Uncover the answer choices and rule out any choices that you know are wrong**. Remember, you are looking for a choice that is closest to the definition that you came up with. Choose the answer that best matched your idea of what the word means.

Now let's go over the answer choices together.

    Ⓐ   keep it

    Ⓑ   confuse it

    Ⓒ   buy it

    Ⓓ   hide it

If you do not know the stem word, rule out as many choices as you can, then guess.

Look at choice A. Does *keep* mean the same as *to conceal*? No, it doesn't. You can rule out answer choice A.

Look at choice B. Does *confuse* mean the same as *to conceal*? No, it doesn't. This is one of those words that might throw you off track. You can rule out answer choice B.

Look at choice C. Does *buy* mean the same as *to conceal*? No, it doesn't. You can rule out answer choice C.

Look at choice D. Does *hide* mean the same as *to conceal*? Yes, it does! Answer choice D is the correct answer.

In the example above, if you did not know the word conceal, you were able to rule out choice B because it looked suspiciously like the stem choice.

Remember to use this technique only if you are certain that you do not know the stem word.

Let's try synonym question #16 from the Practice Test.

16 A <u>tale</u> is —

Ⓕ a story

Ⓖ an animal

Ⓗ a friend

Ⓙ a market

✔ **Even if you don't know the underlined word**, you should read each answer choice and choose the one that you think is the best answer. Sometimes taking your best guess will be all that you can do on the synonym questions.

Let's try synonym question #14 from the practice test.

14 To <u>carve</u> means to—

Ⓕ wait

Ⓖ fix

Ⓗ cut

Ⓙ fill

Here are some more synonym questions for you to try:

1 A <u>gate</u> is a kind of—

Ⓕ flower

Ⓖ beach

Ⓗ door

Ⓙ book

2 A <u>quiz</u> is a kind of—

Ⓐ toy

Ⓑ animal

Ⓒ test

Ⓓ show

3 To <u>rove</u> means to—

Ⓕ punch

Ⓖ name

Ⓗ cut

Ⓙ wander

4 <u>Pleased</u> means—

Ⓐ happy

Ⓑ ugly

Ⓒ complicated

Ⓓ broken

✔ Remember: Cover the answer choices and think of your own definition or synonym first. Even if the first answer seems like the correct choice, be careful and read all the answer choices to be sure.

Multiple Definitions

Some words have more than one meaning. Multiple Definition questions give you a sentence that includes a particular word. That same word is used in a number of different ways in the answer choices. You must find the answer choice in which the word is used in the same way as it is in the first sentence.

This is what a Multiple Definition question looks like:

 Could you throw me that <u>ball</u>?

Which answer uses the word <u>ball</u> in the same way as it is above?

Ⓐ The costume <u>ball</u> is this evening at my friend's house.

Ⓑ I found the <u>ball</u> in the shed in our backyard.

Ⓒ Frank is going to <u>ball</u> up the paper and throw it out.

Ⓓ I had a <u>ball</u> at the party last night!

- **Read the sentence and decide whether the underlined word in the sample sentence is a noun, a verb, or an adjective**. Ask yourself: Is the word a person, place, or thing? If so, it's a *noun*. A *ball* in this case is a round object used for games. It can also mean a kind of dance.

- **Does the word describe something**? If so, it's an *adjective* or *an adverb*. *Ball* in this case describes a feeling of having a good time.

- **Is the word an action**? If so, it's a *verb*. To *ball* something means to roll it up into a round shape.

Helpful Hint

If the sample word is a noun, the answer will be a noun. If the sample word is a verb, the correct answer will be a verb. If the sample word is an adjective, the correct answer will be an adjective.

In the example above, the sample sentence uses the word ball as a noun, meaning the kind of ball that you can play with. Make a mental note of this—it will help you find the correct answer.

Read the sample sentence again. Imagine the item that the sentence describes.

Let's go over the answer choices.

Look at choice *A*. The costume <u>ball</u> is this evening at my friend's house. In this sentence *ball* is a noun. However, in this case it means a kind of dance. You can rule out answer choice *A*.

Look at choice *B*. I found the <u>ball</u> in the shed in our backyard. In this sentence *ball* is a noun, and it's used in the same way as it is in the example. This looks like a good answer. But let's look at all the answer choices before we decide.

Look at choice *C*. Frank is going to <u>ball</u> up the paper and throw it out. In this sentence *ball* is a verb. Since you know that the correct answer must be a noun, you can rule out answer choice *C*.

Look at choice *D*. I had a <u>ball</u> at the party last night! In this sentence *ball* is a noun. However, in this case it means to have a good time. It is a noun, but not the same as the example. You can rule out answer choice *D*. Answer choice *B* is the correct answer.

20 | **The bill at the restaurant was more expensive than I thought.**

Which answer uses the word bill in the same way as it is above?

Ⓕ The plumber sent us a bill for his work.

Ⓖ That bird had a very large bill.

Ⓗ The bill was passed in Congress and became a law.

Ⓙ There were four musicians on the bill that evening.

✔ **Read the sample sentence.** Imagine the thing that the sentence describes. You might think *bill* means *a check*. Remember that as you read through the answer choices.

Since the word *bill* is used as a noun in the sample sentence, the correct answer choice will also use *bill* as a noun.

Let's take a look at the answer choices.

Look at choice *F*. The plumber sent us a <u>bill</u> for his work. In this sentence *bill* is a noun. And it means a check, just like in the example. But, let's look at the other answer choices before we decide.

Look at choice *G*. That bird had a very large <u>bill</u>. In this sentence *bill* is a noun. However, in this case it means *the mouth of a bird*. You can rule out answer choice *G*.

Look at choice *H*. The <u>bill</u> was passed in Congress and became a law. In this sentence *bill* is a noun. However, in this case it means *a future law*. You can rule out answer choice *H*.

Look at choice *J*. There were four musicians on the <u>bill</u> that evening. In this sentence, *bill* is a noun. However, in this case it means *a list of performers*. You can rule out answer choice *J*. Answer choice *F* is the correct answer.

Let's try a few more multiple definition questions.

1 **Could you bend this bar for me?**

Which answer uses the word bend in the same way as it is above?

Ⓐ We saw them coming around the bend.

Ⓑ It's not fair to bend the rules.

Ⓒ The superhero could bend steel with his bare hands!

Ⓓ There's a bend in this straw.

2 **There is a tool shed in back of our house.**

Which answer uses the word back in the same way as it is above?

Ⓕ Back a long time ago, my grandfather played baseball.

Ⓖ I slipped on the ice and fell on my back.

Ⓗ The businessman decided to back the new company.

Ⓙ There's an aquarium at the back of the classroom.

1 | The tree's <u>roots</u> had grown out of the ground.

Which answer uses the word <u>roots</u> in the same way as it is above?

Ⓐ This flower's <u>roots</u> need watering.

Ⓑ He <u>roots</u> for his favorite team.

Ⓒ It's important to get to know your family <u>roots</u>.

Ⓓ We need to get at the <u>roots</u> of these problems.

2 | My father decided to <u>plant</u> tomatoes this year.

Which answer uses the word <u>plant</u> in the same way as it is above?

Ⓕ A lot of people work at the manufacturing <u>plant</u>.

Ⓖ This <u>plant</u> hasn't grown any flowers yet.

Ⓗ If you <u>plant</u> those seeds too late, they won't grow.

Ⓙ Cheryl wanted to <u>plant</u> her surprise gift in Terry's desk.

Words in Context

Words in Context questions ask you to figure out the meaning of an underlined word by looking at the words around it. Many of these words will be new to you, but don't let that bother you. The *context*, or words around the unknown word, will have lots of clues to help you figure out what the word means.

Read this sentence:

The man was <u>confident</u>.

What does confident mean? There is no way to tell from looking at this sentence.

Read this sentence:

The man was so <u>confident</u> that he never thought he was wrong.

The *context*, or words around the underlined word, helps us to figure out what it means. Because the man "never thought he was wrong," you can tell that he is *sure*.

Each Words in Context question on the Reading Vocabulary section of the test will look like this.

 When Billy lost the race, he had a <u>gloomy</u> look on his face.

<u>Gloomy</u> means —

Ⓐ excited

Ⓑ happy

Ⓒ sleepy

Ⓓ sad

To answer this question you should:

- **First read the sentence**. Be sure to cover the answer choices so that they don't confuse you. All of the choices may seem to fit, but only one is correct.

- **Search the sentence for clues**. From the above question, you know that Billy lost the race. Think about what this may mean. How would Billy feel?

- **Based on the clues, try to come up with a substitute for the underlined word**. In this sentence, you might come up with *disappointed*.

Let's take a look at the answer choices.

    Ⓐ   excited

    Ⓑ   happy

    Ⓒ   sleepy

    Ⓓ   sad

Look at choice *A*. Do you think Billy had an *excited* look on his face? That doesn't make sense. Remember, you are looking for a word that means the same as *disappointed*. Does *excited* mean *disappointed*? No, it does not. You can rule out answer choice *A*.

Look at choice *B*. Do you think Billy had a *happy* look on his face? Does *happy* mean *disappointed*? No, it does not. You can rule out answer choice *B*.

Look at choice *C*. Do you think Billy had a *sleepy* look on his face? Does *sleepy* mean *disappointed*? No, it does not. You can rule out answer choice *C*.

Look at choice *D*. Do you think Billy had a *sad* look on his face? Does *sad* mean *disappointed*? Yes, it is close in meaning. Answer choice *D* is the correct answer.

We ruled out wrong answers to find the correct one!

Let's look at context question #24 from The Practice Test:

 24 I made my sister so <u>furious</u> that she would not talk to me for three days. <u>Furious</u> means—

 Ⓕ angry

 Ⓖ happy

 Ⓗ pretty

 Ⓙ tired

✔ **Use the sentence structure to help you figure out the underlined word.** Most context questions are divided into two parts:

- **First part**: gives you the vocabulary word
- **Second part**: describes the vocabulary word

So if a sentence says, Greg was so *desperate that he would do anything to win the race.* The part of the sentence after the word *that* should give you a clue as to what *desperate* means.

Let's try a few more context questions.

1 I need to <u>retrace</u> my steps and figure out what I did yesterday. To <u>retrace</u> means to—

Ⓐ give up

Ⓑ talk about

Ⓒ go over again

Ⓓ walk around

2 After the winter storm, the flower was <u>cased</u> in ice, so we couldn't get it out. <u>Cased</u> means—

Ⓕ covered

Ⓖ called

Ⓗ made

Ⓙ ordered

3 Everyone feels good coming here because it is a <u>shelter</u> for us. A <u>shelter</u> is a place that is—

Ⓐ serious

Ⓑ shy

Ⓒ small

Ⓓ safe

4 When I fell down in the mud, I <u>soiled</u> my brand new clothes. <u>Soiled</u> means —

Ⓕ hairy

Ⓖ dirty

Ⓗ simple

Ⓙ crunchy

READING COMPREHENSION

What is the Reading Comprehension section of the SAT-9?

In this section of the test there are full-page *passages*. Your job is to read the passages and to answer the questions about them. The information that you need to answer the questions can be found in the passage. You just need to look for it.

What are the questions in the Reading Comprehension section like?

- Some of the questions will ask you about *details* of the passage. These answers will probably be easy for you to find in the passage.

- Other questions will ask you to *infer* information. This means you have to use information from the passage to draw a conclusion. The answers to these questions cannot be found directly in the passage. You have to use clues in the passage to answer these questions. To answer these questions, you will need to think like a detective. Using the clues in the passage will help you find the best answer. Remember to rule out answer choices that cannot be correct based on the information in the passage.

- Some questions ask you to think about the *purpose* of the passage. They might ask you what the main idea of the passage is, or they might ask you why the passage was written.

- Another type of question in the Reading Comprehension section asks you to *think about study skills or skills that are needed to do well in school.* Some of these questions ask you to fill in spaces in an outline or map of the passage's events. Others might ask you where to look for more information on the passage.

There are three types of passages in the Reading Comprehension section of the SAT-9:

1. **The first type of passage is like a story.** Usually it is not based on real people or real events, but sometimes it is based on historical events.

2. **The second type of passage tries to teach you about something.** Sometimes these kinds of passages are biographies of historical people. Other times, they talk about how something works. And there are some informational passages which talk about the history of something.

3. **The third type of passage that you might see will look like things that you see in real life.** These kinds of passages can look like advertisements, schedules, instructions, and other everyday things.

Here are three things that you should do to make sure you do your best on the Reading Comprehension section:

Read the passage all the way through first. Don't try to answer the questions before you've read the whole passage—you might not have gotten to the answer yet!

Read the passage carefully. If you read the passage too quickly, you won't be able to understand it completely.

Pay attention to the paragraphs as you read them. After you read a paragraph, you should usually know the answers to all these questions:

- What happened?
- Where did it happen?
- When did it happen?
- Who did it?
- Why did they do it?

What should I do before I answer any questions?

✔ **Look at the sample passage and questions.** The sample will give you an idea of what all the other questions will be like.

✔ **Always read the directions.** Reading the directions only takes a few seconds, but it can save you from choosing a lot of wrong answers.

✔ **Read the questions carefully.** Don't rush to answer them. Sometimes they have important words like *not* or *except*. You can miss these words if you read the question too fast.

Remember!

Read all of the answer choices. You have to find the *best* answer to every question. Some answers may seem like they fit, but if you read all the choices, you will be able to figure out which one fits the *best*.

As with most things, there are steps that you need to follow in order to do your best.

Detail Questions

If someone asked you to describe an apple, what would you say? You might start with how it looks: red skin, white fruit. Then you could describe its smell, its taste, and all of the other things that you think of when you think of an apple. All of these things are *details* about the apple.

Detail questions are questions that ask you to find out something from the passage. They might ask you *what* happened, or *who* did it, or *where* it happened, and so on.

When you have to answer a detail question, you should:

- Figure out what the question is asking you to do.

- Pick out the *key word* from the question. Remember, the *key word* is a word that could be important to answering the question. Sometimes there is more than one key word.

Helpful Hint

Always look for question words— *who, what, when, where, how, why*—when you're trying to decide how to answer a question.

- Scan the passage for the *key word* or for a word that means the same thing as the *key word*.

- Determine if that part of the passage will help you answer the question.

Read this passage from the Practice Test to yourself. Then, look at the question below it.

Railroad schedule

Trains Arriving From			Trains Departing From		
TIME	TRACK	CITY	TIME	TRACK	CITY
10 A.M.	Track 2	Los Angeles	9 A.M.	Track 6	Atlanta
11 A.M.	Track 4	Chicago	10 A.M.	Track 8	Boston
1 P.M.	Track 1	Houston	12 Noon	Track 9	Denver
3 P.M.	Track 5	Denver	2 P.M.	Track 10	Cleveland
4 P.M.	Track 3	New York	4 P.M.	Track 7	Houston
5 P.M.	Track 2	Boston	5 P.M.	Track 6	New York
9 P.M.	Track 4	Cleveland	8 P.M.	Track 8	Chicago

No trains will depart after 8 P.M. due to work to be performed on tracks.

No tickets sold after 7 P.M.

For more information on arriving trains, call 555-3333.

For more information on departing trains, call 555-4444.

1 **What city can you go to, but not come from?**

Ⓐ Los Angeles

Ⓑ Chicago

Ⓒ Atlanta

Ⓓ Cleveland

Let's look at the answer choices

Look at choice *A*. If you look at the Arrivals part of the schedule, you will see that trains do come from Los Angeles at this station. You can rule out answer choice *A*.

Look at choice *B*. If you look at the train schedule, you can see that trains both come from and leave for Chicago. You can rule out answer choice *B*.

Look at choice *C*. The schedule says that there is a train that *goes to* Atlanta, but it does not show any train that *comes from* Atlanta. Answer choice *C* is probably the right answer, but let's take a look at the last answer choice before we decide.

Look at choice *D*. The schedule shows that trains both come from and leave for Cleveland. You can rule out answer choice *D*. Answer choice *C* is the correct answer.

Now answer this question about the same passage on your own.

2 **What city will you go to if you are on the train that leaves at 10 A.M.?**

Ⓕ Los Angeles

Ⓖ Atlanta

Ⓗ Boston

Ⓙ Cleveland

Sequence Questions

Some detail questions will ask you *when* something happened. These questions ask you about the *sequence*, or *order*, of the events in the story. They usually *refer* to another event in the passage. This means that they ask you when something happened in relation to another event in the passage.

If a question contains a time word like first, last, or next, then it is probably a sequence question.

- Figure out what event is being *asked about* in the question.

- Scan the passage for that event.

- Use the time word from the question—*first, last, next*—to find out where the answer is located.

Read this passage to yourself. Then look at the question below it.

When Will It Snow?

Janet sat in her room and looked at the calendar. "Winter vacation has started, and there is no snow." she thought to herself. "How can I ride my new sled if there is no snow?"

For many days now it had been cloudy but warm. When would it ever get cold? What good is a sled if there is no snow?

Janet's Dad told her not to worry. "The weatherman says we may have a big snowstorm tonight," he said. "Tomorrow you can ride your new sled." Janet hoped he was right. She was tired of waiting. That night she went to bed and dreamed of riding her sled in brand new snow.

When Janet woke up in the morning, she ran to the windows to see if it had snowed. At first she could not believe what she saw. Everything was white! There was snow everywhere. Janet got dressed in a hurry and ran downstairs. She grabbed her sled and went into the backyard, and started to climb the big hill there.

At the top of the hill Janet looked down. The backyard looked like soft, white cotton. She jumped on her sled pushed. Down she went! She went down the hill so fast that her hat flew off. When she got to the bottom, she went into a big pile of snow. It felt cold on her neck, but Janet did not care. She was going to ride her new sled all day.

1 **Which of these things did Janet do first?**

Ⓐ She climbed the big hill.

Ⓑ She went to bed.

Ⓒ She looked at the calendar.

Ⓓ She saw snow.

Look at choice *A*. Climbing the big hill is one of the last things Janet did. You can rule out answer choice *A*.

Look at choice *B*. Janet went to bed in the third paragraph. This is not the first thing she did. You can rule out answer choice *B*.

Look at choice *C*. Janet looked at the calendar very early in the passage. This could be the correct answer. But, let's look at the last answer choice before we decide.

Look at choice *D*. Janet saw snow late in the passage. You can rule out answer choice *D*. Answer choice *C* is the correct answer.

Now answer this question about the same passage on your own.

2 **What did Janet see when she woke up?**

Ⓕ rain

Ⓖ the calendar

Ⓗ her sled

Ⓙ snow

Main Idea Questions

Remember when we asked how you would describe an apple? Now think about how you would describe what's *inside* an apple. If you eat an apple, after you bite through the skin and fruit, what are you left with? The core. In a passage, the core is called the *main idea.* The main idea is what everything else in the passage grows from.

When you are reading a passage, you need to chew through all those descriptions and details to get at the main idea. Unlike an apple, though, you shouldn't throw this core away! You're going to need it to answer a lot of your questions.

Here's a sample passage. Read it to yourself now.

Coral Reefs

One of the most beautiful sights in the world is a coral reef. A coral reef is a colony, or group, of special plants and animals living together on top of each other. As each layer dies, the next layer grows on top of it. Full of brightly colored fish and coral, reefs are one of nature's wonders. Coral reefs only grow in warm, shallow, tropical waters.

Coral is the common name for a large group of microscopic plants and animals that have hard, protective shells. The corals build these shells around themselves. As the shells grow, they become part of the shells of the corals around them. Most coral reefs grow less than seven inches per year. As the older corals  die, the new ones build on top of the old shells. In this manner, the reef grows higher as well as wider.

Coral reefs are home to many kinds of sea life. Seaweed, eels, starfish, and sponges can all be found living on or near reefs. The varied shape of a reef, with its tunnels and caves, offers good protection and many different fish will live and hide in coral reefs. These fish are often brightly colored, and the reefs are equally popular with fishermen, divers, and photographers.

1 **What is the main idea of this passage?**

Let's look at the answer choices.

    Ⓐ   to teach you where coral is found

    Ⓑ   to talk about coral reefs

    Ⓒ   to say why coral reefs are popular

    Ⓓ   to tell you how to dive

Look at choice *A*. The passage does say coral is found in tropical waters. However, this is not the main focus of the passage. You can rule out answer choice *A*.

Look at choice *B*. The title of the passage is "Coral Reefs." The passage tells you how the reefs are made, and some important facts about them. This could be a good answer. However, let's look at the other answer choices before we decide.

Look at choice *C*. The passage does say why reefs are popular to dive in. However, this is not the main focus of the passage. You can rule out answer choice *C*.

> # Helpful Hint
>
> **After you've read the whole passage, summarize it.**
>
> If you had to describe the passage in one sentence, how would you do it? This is a great way to find out the passage's main idea.

Look at choice *D*. The passage doesn't tell us anything about how to dive. You can rule out answer choice *D*. Answer choice *B* is the correct answer.

Now you try one on your own. Here's a sample passage. Read it to yourself now.

Growing Mushrooms

You probably know that there are many types of farms. There are farms for plants, cattle, and even chickens. But have you ever heard of a mushroom farm? Well, lots of people around the world work as mushroom farmers. They grow the mushrooms we see in stores. Other people pick wild mushrooms and sell them. Wild mushrooms can be found in woods, fields, and yards. People that pick these mushrooms must be very careful, because many wild mushrooms will make you very sick if you eat them.

All mushrooms need darkness and damp dirt to grow. Mushroom farmers grow mushrooms in caves, cellars, or special rooms. They grow them in a mix of fertilizer, soil, and rotten straw. As the mushrooms grow, the tops, or caps, are picked and sold. The rest of the mushroom is left to grow another cap. This means the farmer can grow several crops before planting again.

Wild mushrooms can grow anywhere. They like areas that are wet and have a lot of shade. Mushrooms can grow in woods, on rotten logs, and even in backyards. One popular mushroom is the truffle. These rare mushrooms only grow underground. To find them people use pigs or dogs that smell the mushrooms and then dig them up.

Mushrooms sold in stores and markets are safe to eat. But you should never eat any mushrooms you find in the woods or in your yard. They are not safe to eat. Growing and picking mushrooms is a job for mushroom farmers.

1 **What is the main idea of this passage?**

   Ⓕ how to pick mushrooms

   Ⓖ how to find truffles

   Ⓗ how mushrooms are grown

   Ⓙ how to eat mushrooms

 Remember to read the passage's title. This can give you a good idea what the passage is going to be about. If a passage is called "Birds In Flight," for example, then it will probably be about birds.

 Pay special attention to the first paragraph. In most passages, the first paragraph is the most important. It sets up the story, and lets you know what the rest of the paragraphs are going to talk about.

Inference Questions

You will not find the answers to all the questions written out in the passages. Some of them will ask you to *infer* information. This means that you have to use the information in the passage to figure out what it suggests.

The correct answer to these kinds of questions can be supported by information in the passage. In a way, it's like taking that apple's skin and fruit and turning it into a pie—the material is all there, you just have to *use* it.

Helpful Hint

If a question uses phrases like you can tell, you can guess, or *probably*, then it's an inference question.

 Remember your main idea. If you know what the passage is about, you will be able draw conclusions about it.

Some inference questions ask you to figure out how a character feels, or what the character likes to do. In order to answer these kinds of questions, you need to look for *character clues*. Character clues are descriptive words which give you an idea of how a character feels or tends to behave.

Read this passage from the Practice Test to yourself. Then, look at the question below it.

The Big Hill

Derek saw the big hill beyond the end of his street every day. No one could miss it. It was so high! You could see everything from up there!

Derek wanted to go up the hill. His older brother and sister had climbed it. But Derek's parents thought he was too young to go up the hill by himself. "You will be old enough soon," Derek's father said. When would soon arrive? Derek could climb the pine tree at the end of the street. Derek could see the whole street from the tree. But the big hill was so much higher!

One day, soon arrived. Derek did well on his last report card. His parents were pleased. They had a surprise for him. They told Derek he was old enough to go up the big hill. "All the way to the top?" Derek asked. "Right to the top," Derek's mother said.

Derek made sure he carried water in his backpack when he left the house. It would be hot climbing the hill. Derek walked to the end of the street. He walked past the pine tree this time. The path started a few steps beyond the pine tree. After a few minutes of walking, the path became steep. Derek was glad he had brought the water. He had to stop and drink several times. He was sweating.

An hour passed. The path led to an area where there were no trees. Derek had reached the top. He looked down at his street. There was his house. It looked so small from up here! There was the supermarket. There was the school. This was better than the pine tree. You really could see everything from up here!

1 **How did Derek probably feel at the end of his trip?**

How do we answer the question? The passage doesn't come right out and tell us how the Derek felt. But, if we read the passage carefully, we should be able to figure the answer.

Let's take a look at the answer choices.

Ⓐ proud

Ⓑ angry

Ⓒ sad

Ⓓ scared

Look at choice A. Derek's goal was to climb the hill. He accomplished his goal. So, he could feel *proud* at the end of his trip. But, let's look at the other answer choices before we decide.

Look at choice B. Nothing in the passage suggests that Derek felt *angry.* You can rule out answer choice *B*

Look at choice C. Nothing in the passage suggests that the Derek felt *sad.* In fact, sad is probably the opposite of what he felt! You can rule out answer choice *C*.

Look at choice D. Nothing in the passage suggests that Derek felt *scared.* You can rule out answer choice *D*. Answer choice *A* is the correct answer.

 Pay attention to descriptive words and phrases in the passage. For example, a passage might not say that a character (let's call him Jack) is happy, but if the passage says "Jack was smiling," you can guess that he is happy.

Now answer this question about the same passage on your own.

 2 **How did Derek feel when he was climbing the hill?**

Ⓕ silly

Ⓖ bashful

Ⓗ tired

Ⓘ bored

Some inference questions ask you to draw conclusions. They may ask you to figure out what might happen next in a story. In addition to character clues, descriptions of setting will help you answer these kinds of questions.

Read this passage to yourself. Then, look at the question below it.

Dog and Cat

One morning Cat was walking down the road when she saw Dog. He was sitting on the sidewalk with a sad look on his face. "Good morning Dog," said Cat. "Why are you sitting here all alone on such a beautiful morning?"

"I have nobody to play with," said Dog. "So I am just sitting here by myself."

"You have nobody to play with?" asked Cat. "How can that be? You have so many friends, and a wonderful boy who lives with you. Where is he this morning?"

"My master is at school," said Dog. "He will be there all day long. I have nobody to play with."

"What about your other dog friends?" asked Cat. She always saw Dog and his friends running up and down the street. "Where are they today?"

"I do not know," said Dog. "I cannot find them this morning. See, I told you I have nobody to play with." Dog shook his head and put his tail between his legs. It seemed that today was going to be a very sad day.

Cat felt bad for Dog. He looked so sad, sitting by the road all alone with nobody to play with. Then she had an idea on how to cheer him up. "I know what you can do," she said to Dog. "You can chase me and try to catch me!"

Dog looked up in surprise. "Do you mean it?" he asked. "You would really let me chase you? But you never play with me. "

"I will play with you today," said Cat. "It will be a fun and special day. You can chase me all day if you want. After all, I am much faster than you are. You will never catch me."

"Yes, that will be fun!" said Dog. Now Dog's tail was wagging back and forth. He had someone to play with after all.

How did Cat think Dog felt at the beginning of the story?

Ⓐ lonely

Ⓑ angry

Ⓒ happy

Ⓓ tired

Look at choice *A*. Cat felt bad for Dog because he was "all alone." This means the same thing as *lonely*. This could be a good answer. But, let's take a look at the other answer choices first.

Look at choice *B*. The passage does not suggest that Cat thought that Dog was angry. You can rule out answer choice *B*.

Look at choice *C*. Cat sees that Dog is "sad." This is the opposite of *happy*. You can rule out answer choice *C*.

Look at choice *D*. The passage does not suggest that Cat thought that Dog was tired. You can rule out answer choice *D*. Answer choice *A* is the correct answer.

✔ **Use descriptions in the passage to determine what is likely to happen.** This is helpful for questions that ask you what might happen after the passage ends. For example, if it is raining when the passage ends, you can guess that Jack won't be going outside to ride his bike.

Now answer this question about the same passage on your own.

 What will probably happen next?

Ⓕ Dog will chase Cat.

Ⓖ Dog will go look for his master.

Ⓗ Cat will chase Dog.

Ⓙ Dog will chase Bird.

Drawing Conclusions

Let's go back to the apple for a second. Say you're eating an apple and your friend comes along. Your friend looks at you funny and asks, *Why are you eating that apple*? You'd probably say, *Because it tastes good!* What your friend just asked you is an analysis question. It's a question that asks *why* something happened.

Read this passage from the Practice Test and look at the question below.

The Liberty Bell

The Liberty Bell is one of the most famous objects from the Revolutionary War. This was the war in which the United States won its independence from the British. The Liberty Bell was used to tell people when something important happened. Remember, it was a time when there was no television or radio. There were newspapers, but they didn't come out every day. At the time, the Liberty Bell was the fastest and easiest way to tell people news. Over the years, it became a symbol for freedom.

The Liberty Bell was made in Pennsylvania. It was first rung in 1752. The bell did not work well when it was first made. In fact, the bell cracked the first time it was used! Copper was added to the bottom of the bell to make it stronger. The bell was used to summon people together for special announcements and events.

Later, the bell was rung for the Boston Tea Party and for the Declaration of Independence. During the war, the British took over Philadelphia. The bell had to be hidden so it would not be captured. The bell was hidden in Allentown, Pennsylvania, underneath the floor of a church. The bell was brought back to Philadelphia when the war was over.

The bell was again used to tell people important news. In 1846, the bell cracked badly when it was rung for George Washington's birthday. It could not be rung again. What should be done with this important part of United States history? A decision was made to put the bell in a museum where everybody could see it. Ever since then, the bell has been on display for the public.

1 **Why was this passage written?**

Ⓐ To show you how to make a bell

Ⓑ To tell you about the Liberty Bell

Ⓒ To talk about Philadelphia today

Ⓓ To discuss the history of bells

Let's take a look at the answer choices.

Look at choice *A*. This passage talks a lot about a specific bell—the Liberty Bell—but it doesn't tell you about how to make one. You can rule out answer choice *A*.

Look at choice *B*. The title of the passage is, "The Liberty Bell." The passage only talks about the Liberty Bell. This is probably the right answer, but let's look at the other answers before we make a decision.

Look at choice *C*. The Liberty Bell is still in Philadelphia, but the passage doesn't talk about Philadelphia today. You can rule out answer choice *C*.

Look at choice *D*. This passage talks about a famous bell, but it doesn't tell you about the history of all bells. You can rule out answer choice *D*. Answer choice *B* is the correct answer.

 Ask yourself: *What can I prove using this passage?* Some questions ask you: *There is enough information in this passage to show that...* You should be able to figure out what the passage suggests and what it doesn't.

Now try another one on your own. Read this passage and answer the questions.

Flea Market

Fun for all ages!

The New City Lion's Club will hold a Flea Market on Saturday, June 21 and Sunday, June 22. The Flea Market will be in the New City Mall parking lot.

The rain dates are June 28 and 29.

The Flea Market opens at 10:00 A.M. and closes at 6:00 P.M.

Jewelry, Crafts, Clothes, Toys, Plants, and many more items will all be for sale. There will be special booths for baby clothes and toys.

Tickets for the flea market will be $2.00 for adults and children over 6 years old. Children 6 and under get in free. No one without a ticket may enter.

If you want to rent a booth, or help at the food booth, please call Mrs. Johnson at 555-1234.

There will be booths selling food, soda, and snacks. Hot coffee and tea will bc free. There will be picnic tables and chairs.

1 This passage was mainly written to—

Ⓐ say who is having a flea market

Ⓑ tell you about a flea market

Ⓒ get you to buy food and soda

Ⓓ say who will be there

2 Why does the flea market need a rain date?

Ⓕ Because there are toys for sale

Ⓖ Because there are booths

Ⓗ Because they will sell food

Ⓙ Because it is outside

3 The author thinks that the flea market is—

Ⓐ wet

Ⓑ cold

Ⓒ fun

Ⓓ boring

Helpful Hint

A *fact* is something that can be proven with evidence. An *opinion* is something that is based on someone's personal feelings.

Fact: Apples grow on trees.

Opinion: This apple tastes good.

Study Skills

Let's say your friend is still asking you about that apple. They ask you, *Where could I go to get an apple like that?* You could tell them the grocery store.

Your friend asked you a *Study Skills* question. A Study Skills question asks you *how* to do something. On the test, the Study Skills questions will ask you *how* to get more information, or *how* you would organize the information you got from the passage.

How do I answer study skills questions?

 Remember the main idea. The main idea will help you come up with the best strategies to answer the questions.

 Know what reference sources are used for what reasons. If a question asks you, *Where could you find the phone number for Ray's Pizza?* the answer probably isn't "thesaurus."

What's in Different Reference Sources

Dictionary: spellings and definitions of words

Encyclopedia: detailed articles on different subjects, in alphabetical order

Telephone Directory: alphabetical listing of phone numbers of homes and businesses

Almanac: short listings of statistical and general information

Thesaurus: listing of synonyms for different words

 Remember reading strategies. Some questions ask you how to answer a previous question. *(In order to answer question #2, you should—)*. Keep in mind what you've already learned about reading passages.

Read this passage and look at the question below.

Little League Awards Dinner

The annual Little League Awards Dinner will be Saturday, October 2, at the Town Youth Center. All tickets will cost $1.00. Little League baseball players get in free.

The schedule will be:

5:00 P.M. Doors open.

5:30 P.M. Dinner is served.

6:30 P.M. Speech by Special Guest—Hall of Fame baseball player Nolan Ryan.

7:00 P.M. Awards are handed out.

8:00 P.M. Awards dinner ends.

After the awards dinner is over there will be sign-up sheets for next season. Parents can also sign up at that time for coaching positions.

For more information, or to order tickets, please call the Little League office at 555-4321.

1 The boxes below show some of the events in the passage above.

Dinner is served		Awards are handed out

Which of these fits the best in box 2?

Let's take a look at the answer choices.

Ⓐ   doors open

Ⓑ   dinner ends

Ⓒ   sign-up for next year

Ⓓ   Nolan Ryan gives speech

Look at choice *A*. The doors open before anything else happens. This can't fit in box 2. You can rule out answer choice *A*.

Look at choice *B*. The dinner ending is the last event of the night. This can't fit in box 2. You can rule out answer choice *B*.

Look at choice *C*. Sign-ups for next year take place after the dinner is over, which is box 3. This can't fit in box 2. You can rule out answer choice *C*.

Look at choice *D*. Nolan Ryan gives a speech between when dinner is served (box 1) and when the awards are handed out (box 3). This can fit in box 2. Answer choice *D* is the correct answer.

Now try a few on your own.

1 **Where would you find a passage like this?**

Ⓐ in a telephone book

Ⓑ on a bulletin board

Ⓒ in a math textbook

Ⓓ in a thesaurus

2 **If you wanted to find out about other awards dinners in your town, you could look—**

Ⓕ in a newspaper

Ⓖ in the dictionary

Ⓗ on a map

Ⓙ in the post office

3 **In which of these books would you most likely find this passage?**

Ⓐ *Famous Dinner Parties*

Ⓑ *How to Have an Awards Dinner*

Ⓒ *Cooking Lessons*

Ⓓ *Local Youth Activities*

A FINAL WORD

You are now ready to take the Reading Vocabulary and Reading Comprehension sections of the Stanford-9 test.

This book has helped you prepare for the test by providing test-taking tips, strategies, and exercises. The practice you've received has made the test more familiar to you. This will help you stay calm during the actual test.

Remember, you've seen and answered these types of questions before. You know how to approach each question type. You can work carefully and confidently.

Rule out wrong answers and take your best guess.

Last but not least: Have fun! That's what learning is all about.